the white rose

Munich 1942–1943

INGE SCHOLL

With an Introduction by DOROTHEE SÖLLE
Translated from the German by ARTHUR R. SCHULTZ

WESLEYAN UNIVERSITY PRESS

WESLEYAN UNIVERSITY PRESS
Published by University Press of New England, Hanover, NH 03755
© 1970, 1983 by Inge Aicher-Scholl
Introduction to the Second Edition © 1983 by Dorothee Sölle

Printed in the United States of America   10   9   8

The first edition of this book was titled *Students Against Tyranny*.
The original German edition was titled *Die Weisse Rose* and was
published in 1952 by Verlag der Frankfurter Hefte GmbH.

The radio broadcast on page 152 herein is translated from:
Deutsche Hörer von Thomas Mann, aus *Reden und Aufsatze II—*
Stockholmer Gesamtausgabe der Werke von Thomas Mann—
copyright © 1965 Katja Mann.

LIBRARY OF CONGRESS CATALOGING IN PUBLICATION DATA
Scholl, Inge, 1917–
    The White Rose.

    Translation of: Die weisse Rose.
    1. Anti-Nazi movement—Germany.   2. Universitat
München—Riot, 1943.   3. Scholl family.   I. Sölle,
Dorothee.   II. Title.
DD256.3.S3362 1983   943.086   83-16828
ISBN 0-8195-6086-3

Contents

Illustrations

Introduction to the Second Edition:
The Legacy of the White Rose

I recall an overcast early spring afternoon when I climbed over the stone wall that separated our garden from our neighbors. I recall my playmate's anxiousness to tell me the news about some university students in Munich who had thrown hundreds of paper sheets from the balcony into the vast entrance hall of the university's main building. (I guess we did not yet know the word "leaflet".) The students were arrested, because the superintendent had seen them do it and promptly notified the police. I was struck by my friend Jürgen's words, as I detested the superintendent of my all girls high school, knowing all too well what kind of power he had. I asked Jürgen what was written on the papers. "Something against the Führer," was his reply. We did not talk about what would happen to these young students, just eight or ten years older than we. Children in Germany in 1943, even if they were as young as we were, knew what would happen. Maybe we fleetingly muttered, "KZ," meaning concentration camp, or "*gleich tot*," meaning killed instantly. I do not remember.

At night my parents would listen to the radio broadcasts from Switzerland and the BBC in London. It might have been then that I first heard the name "White Rose." But it would take two more years of killing and "defending" and gassing before we were freed from Hitler, and many more years before we would start to claim our history and discover that at least some Germans, however few, had resisted the Nazis.

I saw Sophie Scholl's photograph for the first time during one of these seizures of despair most of us are visited by in our youthful years. I remember telling myself that Sophie was the one friend I needed, and would never meet. Why was I still around? How could anyone in my generation, anyone born in 1929, wish to grow up, after all that had happened in our country? Was it not much more natural to stop growing, as Oscar Drummer, in Günter Grass's novel, insisted on doing? We had so few people we could trust in as we entered a world of old Nazis and opportunists. Quite a few former refugees returned to Germany, but we felt as isolated in postwar Germany as Sophie and Hans Scholl and their friends once did.

We heard the White Rose portrayed, after the war, as a group of highly idealistic people with little sense of the realities of power and politics. For many years I believed that this was true. Where was their strategy? Whom did they want to reach? What could they hope for? Was it not clear from the very beginning that they were destined to be caught and to die for a besmirched "fatherland"? Hölderlin—one of the great poets of the idealistic epoch—had said, "For thee, o Fatherland, no one has fallen in vain." Did they not fall in vain? How could one successfully resist Hitler and the military industrial complex of the Alfred Krupps and the I. G. Farbens, armed only with Western political philosophy from Aristotle to Fichte, the words of such classical German writers as Goethe and Schiller, and the wisdom of Lao-tse and the Bible? Sometimes I felt that it was just for us, the next generation, that they had died, preferring death to living under Hitler. I wondered if they died so that we would know there had been at least a few people in Germany, a few students among hundreds of thousands, with a conscience.

I have changed my mind about the so-called youthful "idealism" of the White Rose, and I would like to explain to the North American reader why it is that now in 1983, forty years after these events, I think differently. When I read their material again, I was surprised to find a clear political analysis in the writings of the White Rose. Their leaflets repeatedly underscored the issue which was to be decisive in delaying the downfall of Hitler's Reich—Nazi anti-Communism. Along with anti-Semitism, to which it was linked in many ways, anti-Communism was the most virulent force in the Nazi ideology. Millions of "good" Germans did not like the Nazis, yet thought that they were the lesser evil compared with Communists. These good middle-class Germans, persuaded, by 1933, of the threat of Communism, voted for Hitler, thereby bringing him to power via legal and democratic channels. The conservative Christian parties smoothed Hitler's path to power. Ten years later Germany was a hotbed of robbers and rapists who waged war against all of Europe, while specifically targeting Eastern Europe for their more gruesome atrocities.

The White Rose clearly and justly stated that "the first concern for any German should not be the military victory over Bolshevism, but the defeat of National Socialism." Most good Germans in 1943 did not agree with that statement. Some were blind enough to hope that after a military victory over the Bolsheviks the decent forces in Germany, both military and civil, would oust the Nazi party. Germans had thoroughly assimilated Nazi propaganda on the threat of Bolshevism. Yet the White Rose persisted: "Do not believe in the National Socialist propaganda that chased the terror of Bolshevism into your bones . . ." It is an historical tragedy that the resistance against Hitler inside the military was paralyzed by Stalin's army. Even today, there is little knowledge of the historical facts of the Nazi war against Russia between 1941 and 1945. Many people in Germany (and even more in the United States) do not know who invaded whom in 1941. They do not know that Hitler's army raped and enslaved the Soviet civilian population, nor that they refused to take prisoners of war among Communist functionaries, instead shooting them by order of the Führer. Few are aware that twenty million Soviet citizens died in Hitler's war.

Nazi ideology has taken over the minds of people whenever they consider National Socialism to be the lesser evil as against "the true enemy," Communism, whenever they see this enemy as the well of all evil, as Hitler did. I recall from my childhood the voice of the great German writer Thomas Mann on American radio. He spoke to us—in German—against the crimes of the Nazis, reminding us of our country's democratic and humanistic traditions. A few years later, during the Cold War, Mann said that "anti-Communism is the greatest stupidity of the twentieth century." We have good reasons to recall his statement now.

There is a renewed interest in Hitler's Germany on both sides of the Atlantic. It is the subject of ongoing public discussion, replete with films and television debates, books and articles, discoveries and forgeries. Part of this interest, it must be acknowledged, is fueled by a dangerous, lingering fascination with the demonic personality of Adolf Hitler. But, in my opinion, the new interest in the White Rose goes beyond both legitimate and distorted concerns for the German past. It is rooted in the German political and spiritual situation that arose after December 12, 1979. This date marks a watershed, signaling the end of the post-World War II period. The NATO decision in favor of one of the greatest escalations of the arms race—the deployment of new nuclear missiles on European soil—is seen by many Europeans as the inauguration of a new era—the time before World War III. Since December 1979, millions have marched for peace in the streets of Europe. Thousands in the intellectual, artistic, scientific, and theological communities have asked themselves questions similar to those Sophie and Hans Scholl asked in the forties: What can we do? How far must we tolerate what the superpowers enforce on us? Is it enough to sign petitions, to march in mass rallies in order to try to make the peace movement heard in the media and to influence political leaders? What else can be done?

It is in light of these pressing questions that the new interest in the White Rose surfaces. In their desperate search for role models, the finest members of the younger generation forage into the darkest part of German history. We know that we were militaristic, more so than any other European nation. We set a record for racism through our annihilation of six million Jewish people. We devastated Europe. But is that all there is to remember? Were there not, in addition to the forces of militarism, imperialism, and racism, also the forces of resistance?

The word "resistance" now rings a new bell in Germany. More and more people talk about the necessity of resistance to a military machine which, be it by plan or by accident, may wipe out the two Germanies as the first countries targeted for the Pentagon's strategy of "limited nuclear war." The Pentagon Master Plan, drawn up in the summer of 1982 in response to a White House directive, is the first policy statement of any U.S. administration to proclaim that United States strategic forces must be able to win a protracted nuclear war. What does it mean to resist in this situation? Is there anything we might learn from earlier resisters? It is as if the French word "résistance," which played such an important role in the national identity and destiny of postwar France, finally has come home to Germany as well. How long are we going to tolerate the preparation for war by the deployment of first-strike weapons, whether they be cruise missiles, the MX, or Trident submarines?

Any historical parallels we may draw are not entirely accurate. But it does not require too much imagination to think about what an eighteen-year-old German student today concludes when he or she reads about the White Rose and comes upon phrases like, "Every word which comes from Hitler's mouth is a lie. When he says peace, he means war." What will she think when she reads that? Of whom will he think? In a desperate situation of utter powerlessness, a minority with deep moral and religious convictions has the duty to speak up, and even more, to resist in whatever form necessary.

The political function of a book like this documentation of the White Rose is more than that of providing an accurate historical account. We read history in order not to have to repeat it. When I think about Germany and the brief time in which the White Rose bloomed, I feel choked with shame that there were not more "white roses" in the bleakest hour of my country's history. But shame is, as Karl Marx once said, a revolutionary emotion. The Scholls knew that.

I began this reflection with childhood memories of the Third Reich. I would like to share another memory from a time afterwards. I spent almost ten years of my young adulthood pondering the most important question for my generation. The question was very simple, and we asked it of our fathers and our mothers, our teachers and professors, our textbooks and our culture. The question was related to the Holocaust: How could it have happened? The most terrifying response we got to this question was the most innocent one. People told us that they were unaware of what was happening, that they did not know. I never believed this, and I would not accept this response from anyone. Sometimes I have this nightmare—that my children will later approach me and ask, "Mom, what did you do when Ronald Reagan laid the groundwork for the nuclear Holocaust?" No matter what, I would not be able to say that I did not know. All of us know. We do know, and we have to act in one way or another. That is the legacy of the White Rose.

New York, 1983   —DOROTHEE SÖLLE

The White Rose

In the warm springlike days of early February after the Battle of Stalingrad I was riding in a commuter train from Munich to Solln. Next to me in the railway compartment sat two Party members who were discussing in whispers the latest news from Munich. "Down With Hitler!" had been painted in large white letters on the university walls. Leaflets calling for resistance to the regime had been scattered, and the city had been shaken as if by an earthquake. Everything was still standing; life went on as before; but beneath the surface something had changed. I could tell as much from the conversation of the two men sitting opposite one another in the compartment, putting their heads together. They talked about the end of the war and what they would do when it would suddenly confront them. "The only thing I will be able to do is to shoot myself," said one of them. He glanced quickly in my direction to see whether I had overheard him.

No doubt these two breathed easier when, a few days later, flaming red posters were displayed to calm the populace. They announced:

Sentenced to Death for High Treason:
Christoph Probst, age 24
Hans Scholl, age 25
Sophie Scholl, age 22
The Sentences Have Already Been Carried Out.

The newspapers carried reports of irresponsible lone wolves and adventurers, who by their acts had automatically excluded themselves from the community of the *Volk*. The rumors had spread that up to a hundred persons had been apprehended and that more death sentences could be expected. The president of the People's Court had been flown in expressly from Berlin to execute swift judgment.

In a subsequent court action the following were also condemned and executed:

Willi Graf
Professor Kurt Huber
Alexander Schmorell.

What had these people done? What was their crime?

While some people mocked and vilified them, others described them as heroes of freedom.

But were they heroes? They attempted no superhuman task. They stood up for a simple matter, an elementary principle: the right of the individual to choose his manner of life and to live in freedom. They did not seek martyrdom in the name of any extraordinary idea. They were not chasing after grandiose aims. They wanted to make it possible for people like you and me to live in a humane society. Perhaps their greatness lies in the fact that they committed themselves for the sake of such a simple matter, that they were strong enough to give their lives in defense of the most elementary right. It is perhaps more difficult to stand up for a worthy cause when there is no general enthusiasm, no great idealistic upsurge, no high goal, no supporting organization, and thus no obligation; when, in short, one risks one's life on one's own and in lonely isolation. Perhaps genuine heroism lies in deciding stubbornly to defend the everyday things, the trivial and the immediate, after having been bombarded with so much oratory about great deeds.

The tranquil town in the Kochertal where we lived as

children seemed forgotten by the world. Our only communication with the outside was the yellow mail coach that carried us over a long, bumpy road to the railroad station. But my father, the mayor, was disturbed by the inconvenience of our isolation, and finally he prevailed over the conservative local farmers in a long struggle to build a branch line connecting us with the railway.

To us children, however, the world of this little town was not narrow, but rich, great, and splendid. We also soon learned that the world did not end at the horizon where the sun rose and set, and one day the wheels of our beloved railway carried us and all our belongings far away across the Swabian Jura.

We had taken a great leap when we got off the train in Ulm, that city on the Danube which was henceforth to be our home. Ulm—the name sounded to us like the boom of the biggest bell in its mighty cathedral. At first we were homesick, of course, but soon new things captured our attention, in particular the *Höhere Schule* (secondary school) in which the five of us were enrolled in turn.

One morning I heard a girl tell another on the steps of the school, "Now Hitler has taken over the government." The radio and newspapers promised, "Now there will be better times in Germany. Hitler is at the helm."

For the first time politics had come into our lives. Hans was fifteen at the time, Sophie was twelve. We heard much oratory about the fatherland, comradeship, unity of the *Volk*, and love of country. This was impressive, and we listened closely when we heard such talk in school and on the street. For we loved our land dearly—the woods, the river, the old gray stone fences running along the steep slopes between orchards and vineyards. We sniffed the odor of moss, damp earth, and sweet apples whenever we thought of our homeland. Every inch of it was familiar and

5

dear. Our fatherland—what was it but the extended home of all those who shared a language and belonged to one people. We loved it, though we couldn't say why. After all, up to now we hadn't talked very much about it. But now these things were being written across the sky in flaming letters. And Hitler—so we heard on all sides—Hitler would help this fatherland to achieve greatness, fortune, and prosperity. He would see to it that everyone had work and bread. He would not rest until every German was independent, free, and happy in his fatherland. We found this good, and we were willing to do all we could to contribute to the common effort. But there was something else that drew us with mysterious power and swept us along: the closed ranks of marching youth with banners waving, eyes fixed straight ahead, keeping time to drumbeat and song. Was not this sense of fellowship overpowering? It is not surprising that all of us, Hans and Sophie and the others, joined the Hitler Youth.

We entered into it with body and soul, and we could not understand why our father did not approve, why he was not happy and proud. On the contrary, he was quite displeased with us; at times he would say, "Don't believe them—they are wolves and deceivers, and they are misusing the German people shamefully." Sometimes he would compare Hitler to the Pied Piper of Hamelin, who with his flute led the children to destruction. But Father's words were spoken to the wind, and his attempts to restrain us were of no avail against our youthful enthusiasm.

We went on trips with our comrades in the Hitler Youth and took long hikes through our new land, the Swabian Jura. No matter how long and strenuous a march we made, we were too enthusiastic to admit that we were tired. After all, it was splendid suddenly to find common interests and allegiances with young people whom we might otherwise not have gotten to know at all. We attended

6

evening gatherings in our various homes, listened to readings, sang, played games, or worked at handcrafts. They told us that we must dedicate our lives to a great cause. We were taken seriously—taken seriously in a remarkable way—and that aroused our enthusiasm. We felt we belonged to a large, well-organized body that honored and embraced everyone, from the ten-year-old to the grown man. We sensed that there was a role for us in a historic process, in a movement that was transforming the masses into a *Volk*. We believed that whatever bored us or gave us a feeling of distaste would disappear of itself. One night, as we lay under the wide starry sky after a long cycling tour, a friend—a fifteen-year-old girl—said quite suddenly and out of the blue, "Everything would be fine, but this thing about the Jews is something I just can't swallow." The troop leader assured us that Hitler knew what he was doing and that for the sake of the greater good we would have to accept certain difficult and incomprehensible things. But the girl was not satisfied with this answer. Others took her side, and suddenly the attitudes in our varying home backgrounds were reflected in the conversation. We spent a restless night in that tent, but afterwards we were just too tired, and the next day was inexpressibly splendid and filled with new experiences. The conversation of the night before was for the moment forgotten. In our groups there developed a sense of belonging that carried us safely through the difficulties and loneliness of adolescence, or at least gave us that illusion.

Hans had learned a repertory of songs, and his troop enjoyed hearing him sing to his own guitar accompaniment. He sang not only the songs of the Hitler Youth but also folksongs of many countries and peoples. What a magical effect the singing of a Russian or Norwegian song could produce with its gloomy, impelling melancholy. How much it told about these peoples and their lands.

But after a time Hans underwent a remarkable change; he became a different person. Some disturbing element had entered his being. This had nothing to do with Father's objections; he was able to close his ears to those. It was something else. The leaders had told him that his songs were not allowed, and when he made light of this prohibition, they threatened punishment. Why should he be forbidden to sing these songs that were so full of beauty? Merely because they had been created by other races? He could see no sense in it; he was depressed, and his light-hearted manner disappeared.

At this time he was honored with a very special assignment. He was chosen to be the flagbearer when his troop attended the Party Rally in Nuremberg. His joy was great. But when he returned, we could not believe our eyes. He looked tired and showed signs of a great disappointment. We did not expect any explanation from him, but gradually we found out that the image and model of the Hitler Youth which had been impressed upon him there was totally different from his own ideal. The official view demanded discipline and conformity down to the last detail, including personal life, while he would have wanted every boy to follow his own bent and give free play to his talents. The individual should enrich the life of the group with his own contribution of imagination and ideas. In Nuremberg, however, everything was directed according to a set pattern. Day and night the talk was about *Treue*—loyalty. But what was the foundation of *Treue*, after all, but being true to oneself? Rebellion was stirring in Hans's mind.

Soon afterward a new prohibition upset him. One of the leaders snatched out of his hands a book by his favorite author, *Sternstunden der Menschheit* by Stefan Zweig. It was banned, he was told. But why? There was no answer. A similar judgment was pronounced against another German

8

Hans Scholl, Ulm, born September 22, 1918, medical student, executed
February 22, 1943

author whom Hans liked very much. This man had had to flee Germany because he had defended the idea of peace.

Finally the open break came.

Some time before, Hans had been promoted to the rank of *Fahnleinführer*—troop leader. He and his boys had sewn a handsome banner, bearing in its design a great mythical beast. This flag was something special; it was dedicated to the Furhrer, and the boys had pledged their loyalty to the banner because it was the symbol of their fellowship. One evening, however, when they had come into formation with their banner and stood in review before a higher-echelon leader, the unheard-of happened. The leader suddenly and without warning ordered the little flagbearer, a cheerful twelve-year-old, to hand over the banner.

"You don't need a banner of your own. Use the one prescribed for everyone."

Hans was deeply disturbed. Since when this rule? Didn't the cadre leader know what this particular flag meant to the troop? After all, it was not just another piece of cloth that could be changed at will.

The order to hand over the banner was repeated. The boy stood rigid, and Hans knew how he felt and that he would refuse. When the order was given for the third time, in a threatening voice, Hans noticed that the flag was trembling. At that he lost control. He quietly stepped from his place in the ranks and slapped the cadre leader.

That put an end to Hans' career as *Fähnleinführer*.

The spark of tormenting doubt which was kindled in Hans spread to the rest of us.

In those days we heard a story about a young teacher who had unaccountably disappeared. He had been ordered to stand before an SA squad, and each man was ordered to pass by the teacher and to spit in his face. After that incident no one saw him him again. He had disappeared into a concentration camp. "What did he do?" we asked his mother in bewilderment. "Nothing. Nothing," she cried out in despair. "He just wasn't a Nazi, it was impossible for him to belong. *That* was his crime."

Oh God, at that the doubts which had arisen soon turned to deep sadness and then burst into a flame of rebellion. Within us the world of purity and faith was crumbling, bit by bit. What was really happening to our fatherland? No freedom, no flourishing life, no prosperity or happiness for anyone who lived in it. Gradually one bond after another was clamped around Germany, until finally all were imprisoned in a great dungeon.

"Father, what is a concentration camp?"

He told us what he knew and suspected and added: "That is war. War in the midst of peace and within our own people. War against the defenseless individual. War against human happiness and the freedom of its children. It is a frightful crime."

But perhaps the tormenting disappointment was only a bad dream, from which we would awaken in the morning. In our hearts arose a violent struggle. We tried to defend our old ideals against everything we had seen and heard.

"But does the Führer have any idea of the concentration camps?"

"How could he not know, since they've existed for years and were set up by his closest friends? And why didn't he use his power to do away with them at once? Why are those who are released from them forbidden on pain of death to tell anything about what they went through?"

There awoke in us a feeling of living in a house once beautiful and clean but in whose cellars behind locked doors frightful, evil, and fearsome things were happening. And as doubt had slowly taken hold of us, so now there grew within us a horror and a fear, the first germ of unbounded uncertainty.

11

"But how is it possible that in our country a thing like this could take over the government?"

"In a time of great troubles," explained Father, "all sorts come to the surface. Just recall the bad times we had to live through: first the war, then the difficult postwar years, inflation, and great poverty. Then came unemployment. If a man's bare existence is undermined and his future is nothing but a gray, impenetrable wall, he will listen to promises and temptations and not ask who offers them."

"But after all, Hitler did keep his promise to do away with unemployment."

"No one denies that. But don't ask about his methods! He started up the munitions industry, he's building barracks. Do you know where that will lead? He could have eliminated unemployment by means of peacetime industries—in a dictatorship that can easily be managed. But surely we are not like cattle, satisfied if we have fodder for our bellies. Material security alone will never be enough to make us happy. After all, we're human beings, with free opinions and our own beliefs. A regime which would tamper with these things has lost every spark of respect for man. Yet that is the first thing which we must demand from it."

This talk between Father and ourselves occurred on a long hike in the spring. Once again we had thoroughly talked out our questions and doubts.

"What I want most of all is that you live in uprightness and freedom of spirit, no matter how difficult that proves to be," he added.

Suddenly we were comrades, our father and ourselves, and none of us were conscious that he was so much older. We had the welcome sensation of seeing our horizons widen, and at the same time we understood that this expansion of the world brought with it danger and risk.

12

Now our family was a small, stable island in the ever stranger, incomprehensible swirl of events.

But along with this feeling there was something else for Hans and my youngest brother Werner, something which gave shape to their lives in the years between fourteen and eighteen and which filled them with indescribable high spirits. That was their association with a small group of friends in the *Jungenschaft*—an organization which existed in various German cities, particularly where the cultural life was still active. It was the last remaining splinter of the disbanded *Bündische Jugend* and had actually long since been outlawed by the Gestapo. The club had its own most impressive style, which had grown up out of the membership itself. The boys recognized one another by their dress, their songs, even their way of talking. I do not know whether such a phenomenon can be described at all; it has to be experienced at first hand. For these boys life was a great, splendid adventure, an expedition into an unknown, beckoning world. On weekends they went on hikes, and it was their way, even in bitter cold, to live in a tent such as the Lapps used in the Arctic. Seated around the campfire they would read aloud to each other or sing, accompanying themselves with guitar, banjo, and balalaika. They collected the folksongs of all peoples and wrote words and music for their own ritual chants and popular songs. They painted and took photographs, wrote and composed—and out of the results they put together their magnificent and inimitable "Excursion Books" and magazines. In winter they climbed the most remote meadow slopes and skied down the most daring breakneck runs. They loved to practice with their foils in the early dawn. They carried certain favorite books that opened to them new dimensions of the world and of their inner selves. They were solemn and silent; with their own peculiar sense of humor they had whole buckets of sarcasm, mockery, and skepticism. They

13

would race through the woods in wild, unrestrained excitement; plunge into ice-cold rivers during early mornings; then for hours on end lie on their stomachs watching the game and the wildfowl. At concerts they would sit just as still, with bated breath, drinking in the music. If a good film happened to be in town, they turned up at the movies, or in the theater when a play aroused their interest. They explored the museums and were well acquainted with the cathedral and its most inaccessible splendors. In a special way they loved the blue horses of Franz Marc, the vibrant fields and suns of van Gogh, and the exotic world of Gauguin. But none of this conveys anything precise. And perhaps it is better not to be precise, because they themselves were so uncommunicative as they quietly grew into adulthood, into life.

One of their favorite songs went:

Close eye and ear a while
Against the tumult of the time;
You'll not still it or find peace
Until your heart is pure.

As you watch and wait
To catch the Eternal in the Everyday,
You freely choose to take your role
In History's great play.

The hour will come when you are called.
Be then prepared, be ready;
If the fire dies down, leap in;
Again it blazes, steady.

Suddenly there occurred throughout Germany a wave of arrests that wiped out these last remnants of a genuine youth movement which had started at the beginning of the century with high expectations and great spirit.

14

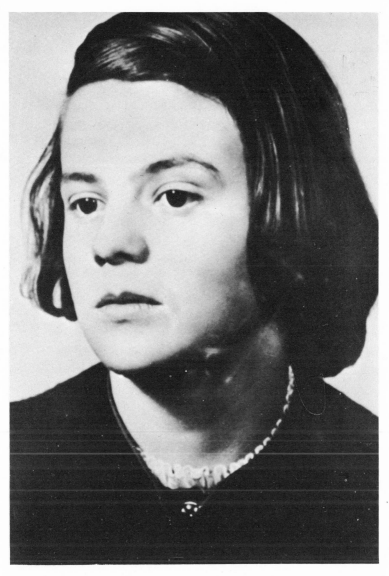

Sophie Scholl, Ulm, born May 9, 1921, biology and philosophy student, executed February 22, 1943

For many of these young men imprisonment was one of the great fruitful shocks of their young years. Many of them understood now that youth, the movement, and the club had to come to an end, that they had to step into adult life. The diaries, magazines, and songbooks were seized and reduced to pulp. After weeks or months of prison the young men were released. At that time Hans wrote on the flyleaf of one of his favorite books: "Tear out our hearts—and they will fatally burn you."

The time of youth would have had to end in any case, even without the Gestapo. Hans came to this realization as soon as he was face to face with the gray prison walls. Now he concentrated on his forthcoming education and decided to enter the field of medicine.

Hans was aware that beauty, esthetic pleasure in existence, and his passive growth to manhood were no longer enough, that these could no longer insulate him from the dangers of the times. He felt that there was at bottom an acute emptiness and that there were no answers to his difficult, profound, and disquieting questions; not in Rilke and not in Stefan George, not in Nietzsche nor in Hölderlin. But he was sure that his honest search would lead him along the right path. Finally, by strange detours, he made the acquaintance of the ancient Greek philosophers, Plato and Socrates. He stumbled upon the early Christian philosophers and occupied himself with the great St. Augustine. He discovered Pascal. The Bible took on a new and startling meaning; a sense of immediacy broke through the old and apparently worn-out words, giving them the authority of persuasive reality.

Years had passed meanwhile. The war within the country, against single individuals, had turned into the war against the nations, had become the Second World War.

Hans had already started at the university when the war broke out. For the time being he had been allowed to

16

continue. Then he was drafted into a company of medics, and soon thereafter he took part in the campaign in France. Later he was able to continue his studies, being assigned to a student company in Munich. It was an unusual kind of life—half soldier, half student, sometimes in the barracks, at other times at the university or the hospital—two opposing ways of life, which he was not able to reconcile. This split existence was difficult enough, but the heavier and gloomier burden he had to bear was that he lived in a country where bondage, hatred, and falsehood had become the normal mode of existence.

The viselike rule of naked force was becoming tighter and ever more unbearable. Each day of liberty was a gift, for no one was secure against arrest; one might be arrested in the street, because of some trivial remark, and disappear, perhaps for ever. Would he be surprised if tomorrow morning the Gestapo were to come to his door and put an end to his freedom?

Hans knew, of course, that he was but one of millions in Germany who felt as he did. But woe to him who dared to speak freely and openly. He would surely be shipped off to prison. Woe to the mother who gave vent to her feelings and cursed the war. It would be a long time before she could enjoy life again. All of Germany was spied upon, and secret ears listened everywhere.

On several occasions in the spring of 1942 we found hectographed letters in our mailbox. These carried excerpts from the sermons of Count Galen, Bishop of Münster, and they radiated an astonishing aura of courage and integrity.

All Münster lives under the impression of the frightful destruction the external enemy has inflicted upon us during the past week. Yesterday, the twelfth of July, at the end of this week, the Gestapo confiscated the

17

two monasteries of the Society of Jesus in our city. They have driven the residents out of their properties and have ordered the priests and brothers on that same day, not only to vacate their houses, but also to leave the states of Westphalia and the Rhineland. The same hard judgment was meted out yesterday to the sisters. The residences and properties, together with all household goods, have been made over to the office of the Gauleiter for Northern Westphalia.

Thus the attack on the convents and monasteries, which for some time now has raged in the Eastern Provinces, in southern Germany, in the newly won areas of the Warthegau, Luxemburg, Lorraine, and other parts of the Reich, has begun here in Westphalia as well.

What will come of this? It is not a matter of providing temporary shelter for the homeless people in Münster. The brothers in the order were ready and determined to give up, if necessary, their residences, to take in the homeless, as other people do, and to provide them with food. No, this was not the problem. I have heard that the Gau film center is to be set up in the Convent of the Immaculate Conception in Wikinghege. I have been told that a lying-in hospital for unmarried mothers is to be installed in the Benedictine Abbey of St. Joseph. To date no newspaper has carried stories about the bloodless victories won by the Gestapo officials over defenseless brothers and helpless German women, nor of the conquests which the Gauleiters have made of the goods of their German fellow citizens. Verbal protests and telegrams are in vain.

We cannot take arms against the internal enemy who torments and conquers us. For us there is but one weapon: strong, tenacious, and firm steadfastness. Become strong! Remain unshaken! Now we see clearly

18

and learn quite explicitly what lies at the bottom of the new teaching to which we have been forced to listen all these years and for the sake of which religious instruction has been banned from the schools; which has suppressed our organizations and is now about to destroy the nursery school. It amounts to a deep-running hatred of Christianity, which is scheduled to be rooted out.

At this moment we are not the hammer but the anvil. Others, most of whom are outsiders and apostates, are hammering upon us. They have set about by force to reshape our people and even our youth, to turn them away from God. What they are now forging is illegal imprisonment, exile and expulsion of the innocents. But God will stay by their side, to help them maintain the form and spirit of Christian fortitude as the hammer of persecution strikes them bitterly and wounds without cause.

For some months now we have been hearing that mental patients who have been ill for a long time and are apparently incurable have been removed from the hospitals by force, on orders from Berlin. Regularly the relatives are informed after a short while that the patient has died, the body has been cremated, and the ashes may be called for. There is a widespread suspicion, verging on certainty, that the many unexpected deaths among mental patients have not been due to natural causes but have been deliberately arranged and that the officials follow the precept that it is permissible to destroy "life which does not deserve to live"—to kill innocent persons, if it is decided that such lives are no longer of value to the *Volk* and the state. It is a terrible doctrine, which excuses the murder of innocent people, which gives express licence to kill unemployable invalids, cripples, incurables, and the seniles and those who suffer from incurable disease!

Upon reading these pages, Hans was deeply agitated. "Finally a man has had the courage to speak out." Abstractedly he studied the leaflets and said after a while; "We really ought to have a duplicating machine."

In spite of everything, Hans' great joy in life could not be easily quenched. Indeed, the darker the world about him became, the brighter and stronger grew this power within him, and it increased and was strengthened after his experience of the war in France. Through such familiarity with death life took on a special value.

In those days Hans was exceptionally lucky in the acquaintances he made. On a sunny day in autumn he met the gray-haired editor of a well-known journal which the Nazis had banned. Hans just happened to go to his house on a casual errand; but the old man's bright eyes looked intently at Hans, and after the man had exchanged a few words with him, he was invited to return. From then on Hans was a daily visitor. For hours on end he ranged through the immense library, the gathering ground of poets, scholars, and philosophers. A hundred doors and windows into the world of the mind opened in converse with them. But he saw also that they existed like underground plants in this state of bondage and that all of them expressed the same great yearning: to breathe freely again, to be able to work in freedom and to be entirely themselves.

Among the students Hans also met some who shared his sentiments. One especially among them caught his attention because of his tall figure and his totally unmilitary, elegant, and carefree bearing. This was Alexander Schmorell, son of a well-known Munich physician. Soon a close friendship developed between them, starting from the instinctive unanimity with which the two of them were always ready to disrupt the dull barracks life with their practical jokes and clever tricks. There can be few men who had Alex's radiant, relaxed humor. He beheld the world with eyes full of imagination—it was as if he saw it anew each day. He found the world beautiful, fresh, and filled with captivating delights, and he enjoyed it in an open, childlike way, without questioning or calculating. He was at once totally receptive and unstintingly generous, dispensing gifts royally. Sometimes, however, there appeared behind his cheerful, untrammeled manner something else—a questioning and seeking, an ancient, deep-seated seriousness. He had come to Germany as an infant, brought by his parents from Russia.

Soon after, through Alex, Hans made another friend among the students—Christl Probst. Hans recognized at once that there was a bond between him and Christl: the same love of nature and all creation, the same response to books and writers. Christl had studied the stars and knew a great deal about the minerals and plants of the mountains of upper Bavaria, where he lived. His strongest tie with Hans, however, was their common search for the principle underlying all phenomena, underlying man and man's history. Christl admired and greatly respected his late father, a self-taught scholar. It may be that his father's early death accounted in large measure for Christl's exceptional maturity. He alone of the group of students was married; he had two sons, aged two and three. For this reason he was carefully excluded from political acts which might bring him into danger. Later a fourth student joined the group— Willi Graf, a tall, blond boy from the Saar region. He was a rather taciturn fellow, thoughtful and reserved. When Hans got to know him, it was immediately evident that Willi belonged with them. He too was occupied intensely with problems of philosophy and theology. Sophie described him: "When he says anything, in his very deliberate way, one has the impression that he would not speak unless he could commit himself with his whole being. That's why everything about him gives the impression of being precise, genuine, and wholly reliable." Willi's father, the head of a large business firm, was accustomed to having his son go his own way. Early in life Willi had joined a Catholic youth club, and the wave of arrests which in 1938 had caught up Hans had also involved Willi. Now he, along with Christl, Alex, and Hans, was studying medicine.

After a concert they would meet in an Italian wine shop, but they soon came to feel very much at home in Hans' room or at Alex's house. They would recommend books to one another, read aloud, and hold discussions, but sometimes they would suddenly be seized by wild high spirits and invent all sorts of nonsense. Their excess of imagination, humor, and love of life had to be given vent from time to time.

It was the eve of Sophie's twenty-first birthday.

"It seems almost unbelievable that I'll be able to start at the university tomorrow," she had said to her mother on saying good night. Her mother, ironing, stood in the hall, on the floor next to her an open suitcase with clothes and fresh linen and all the little things that Sophie would need in her new life as student. Alongside stood a handbag containing a crisp, brown, sweet-smelling cake. Sophie bent down and sniffed it. And there, next to it, she discovered a bottle of wine! Sophie had had to wait a long time for this day.

It had been a difficult test of patience. First came half a year of labor service that seemed endless. Then, when she was ready to leap eagerly into a life of freedom, a new obstacle arose: a further half-year of war-aide service. She hated to be emotional about it, but how she had suffered! She had never been afraid of work, but she disliked what

22

went with it: working under orders, being herded together with the others in the camps; the deadly standardization. But these could still be borne if necessary, had not her convictions forced her into a state of continuous resistance. Wasn't it an unforgivable sign of weak character if she gave the least bit of service to a state founded on lies, hatred, and bondage? "I want you to live in uprightness and freedom of spirit," her father had said. How unutterably difficult that could be! Sometimes Sophie had felt that this conflict was unbearable, and she isolated herself from the girls in the labor service. She kept in the background and tried to give the impression of not being there at all. Let the other girls think what they pleased. So she learned to know homesickness and loneliness. She had held onto two things from home, however, from the other world; they were like moorings in this sea of strangeness and senselessness. The one was the need—perhaps it was a protection against a hostile environment—to care for her body with special pains. For the other, her spirit sought support in the thoughts of St. Augustine. It was strictly forbidden to keep one's own books, but Sophie's volume of St. Augustine was hidden in a safe place. In those years there was a renaissance of theological literature, ranging from the early Church fathers to the scholastics, with St. Thomas Aquinas as the central figure, and it embraced also their bold successors in modern French philosophy and theology. This renaissance had also attracted certain groups standing outside the established faiths. In Augustine Sophie discovered words written, as it seemed, just for her and which suited her exactly, though they were already a thousand years old: "Thou madest us for Thyself, and our heart is restless until it reposes in Thee." *

---

*Confessions, I, 1. Trans. by Edward B. Pusey (New York, Modern Library).

No, this state was not the same as a child's homesickness. It was much more, and Sophie sometimes had the feeling that the world was an infinitely strange, empty, and God-forsaken void. Through specialization and organization men had developed the capacity to build the delicately complex structure of civilization. But again and again they denied their being and destroyed each other's achievements—in the end not only their works, but themselves as well.

Sophie had discovered a small chapel near the camp and had visited it at times. It had been pleasant to sit at the organ and play, or to idle and daydream, listening to the sounds of nature. Then her shattered world was gently rebuilt and took on a sense of order and meaning. In her free time she slipped out into the large park surrounding the camp, with its encircling woods and meadows. There she had lain very still, herself a tiny part of the natural order. How beautiful was the outline of a fir tree; how undisturbed and calmly a tree like this lived out its time. How beautiful the moss on the trunk, nourishing itself on the tree with such easy dependence. Life—how immense and how hard to grasp. Sophie felt that her skin had become smooth and absorbent, as if it could inhale the magic, lovely existence of these objects. But then the inner conflict would burst forth again and draw all the world with it into her sorrow.

But for the moment she was free. Tomorrow she would travel to Munich. She would take charge of her life, go to the university, to Hans.

Her mother was still standing at her ironing, carefully smoothing a blouse. Now this girl too had grown up and was old enough to leave home—her youngest, her stubborn little one. What would the future bring her? A wave of hope engulfed her mother's thoughts. Sophie would manage, no matter where she went. She had always succeeded, no

24

matter what she had set out to do. Mother's thoughts wandered on, about each child in turn. She paused in thinking about her youngest boy, now in Russia. What was he doing at that moment? If only the war were over, and they were all gathered at home around the table! Mother knelt down and closed the suitcase. "They are in God's care," she said as she turned to put the things away. Meanwhile she hummed a song, noticing with a start that it was the lullaby with which she had often sung the children to sleep: "Spread wide your wings . . . ."

At times Mother's tranquil heart was torn by a great unaccustomed worry; some time ago, in the early morning, the doorbell had rung and three men from the Gestapo had come to speak with Father. First they held a lengthy conversation with him, and then they searched the house. When they left, they took Father with them. On that day we realized fully, in our very bones, that we were horribly helpless. What did a single individual matter in this state? He was a speck of dust, to be flicked away with a finger. It was only through great good fortune—like a miracle—that Father was released. But it was impressed upon him that his "case" was not yet cleared. My father had been denounced by an employee to whom he had incautiously betrayed his private opinion of Hitler. The woman had heard him call Hitler God's scourge of mankind.

What would happen now? Sometimes we had hopes that everything would be all right in the end. However, an icy, tormenting feeling would grip our hearts, as if the paw of a monstrous beast was poised over us, ready to descend at any moment. And no one knew who the next victim would be.

"This child shall come to no harm," sang Mother as she finished her song. Today Sophie's joy and the busy preparations for her departure elbowed these troubles out of her mind.

I still see her as she stood before me, my sister, on the following morning, ready to start and full of expectation. At her temple she wore a yellow daisy, retrieved from the birthday table. It was beautiful to see her dark, smooth, shiny hair hang down to her shoulders. With her large brown eyes she looked upon the world critically but with lively interest. Hers was still a child's face, with delicate features. In it there was something akin to the nervous curiosity of a young animal and at the same time an expression of great seriousness.

When her train rolled at last into the Munich station, she spied her brother's cheerful face at a distance. In an instant everything was familiar and easy again. "Tonight you'll meet my friends," said Hans; he was tall and self-assured as he walked beside Sophie.

In the evening they met in Hans' room. Next to Sophie, her birthday cake was the focus of their welcome. It was an almost illicit rarity in those years. Someone suggested that they read poems aloud and let the others guess the author. Everybody was fascinated by this game. "But now I've got a really hard puzzle for you," said Hans excitedly, as he fished a typewritten sheet from his wallet. He read:

From his dark den there comes
A robber to waylay us;
He wants to snatch our purses,
But finds a better booty:
A quarrel over nothing,
Confused and ignorant rant,
A nation's banner torn,
A people dull and stupid.

Wherever he goes he finds
The times are lean and empty,

26

So he can step forth brazenly
And play the role of prophet.
He boldly plants his foot
On the rubbish heap around him
And hisses his venal message
To an astonished world.

Cloaked in deceit and malice,
That wrap him like a cloud,
He stands before the people,
The mightiest in the land.
The hands of many helpers
Of low and high degree,
Espying their advantage,
Bring service to his will.

They carry forth his message
As formerly the angels
Had done with the five loaves.
It rattles on and on!
Where once but one man lied,
Today they come by thousands:
And roaring like the storm,
His gold draws interest now.

It grows to a great harvest.
The social order overthrown,
The masses live in infamy
And laugh at every scurvy deed.
It turns out to be true,
What first was fabrication:
The good have disappeared,
The bad come out in crowds!

When one day this trouble
Will melt like winter's ice,
The people will recall it

Like the very Plague itself.
They'll raise an effigy of straw;
Let children on the heath
Burn joy from out of sorrow,
And light from ancient woe.*

For a moment all were silent. "That's excellent," said Christl in amazement.

"Tremendous, Hans; you ought to dedicate that to the Führer. It ought to be printed in the *Volkischer Beobachter*," said Alex in delight over the double import of the verses. "I wonder who wrote that poem?"

"It was written a hundred years ago by Gottfried Keller."

"All the better; we can print it without having to pay royalties: we can drop it from planes all over Germany."

Sophie reminded them of the wine. Alex suggested that they chill it in the English Garden. "Just look at that moon, huge and golden yellow like a beautiful fried egg. We've got to go out and enjoy it." They went into the park and in their hilarity drew the bottle on the end of a long string through the cold waters of the Isar. Alex had brought his balalaika and began to sing. Hans took up his guitar, and Willi whistled through his fingers. All at once they were singing happily and wildly, like persons under a spell.

Sophie spent the night at her brother's. She was still thinking about the events of the evening. At first the stu-

---

*Hans quotes six stanzas (omitting the first) of "Die öffentlichen Verleumder" ("Public Slanderers") by the Swiss poet Gottfried Keller (1819–1890). This is a political jeremiad addressed to the citizens of Zurich. It refers to an incident which occurred in 1878, the hounding and persecution in the public press of the director of the Zurich hospital for mental patients. — ARS

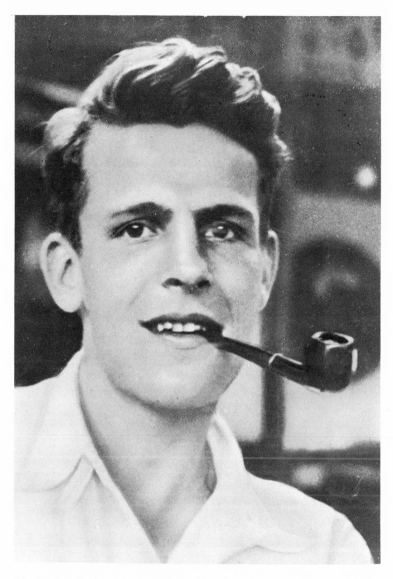

Christoph Probst, born November 6, 1919, medical student, executed February 22, 1943

dents had talked about their work in the hospitals and first-aid stations, to which they had been assigned during the vacations. "There's nothing more pleasant than going from bed to bed and having the sense of holding in your hands a life in peril. There are moments when I'm absolutely happy," Hans had said.

"But isn't it preposterous," somebody interrupted, "that we sit in our rooms and study how to heal mankind when on the outside the state every day sends countless young people to their death? What in the world are we waiting for? Until one day the war is over and all nations point to us and say that we accepted this government without resisting?"

All at once the word *resistance* had been uttered. Sophie could not remember who had used it first. In all the countries of Europe it was springing to life as the result of the suffering, anguish, and oppression that followed on the heels of Hitler's conquests.

Even as she was falling asleep, the verses by Gottfried Keller kept running through her thoughts, and half in a dream she saw a blue sky over Germany filled with fluttering leaflets spiraling to the ground. Suddenly she heard Hans say, "We must get hold of a duplicating machine."

"What?"

"Oh, forget you heard me, Sophie dear. I didn't mean to wake you."

Through a young Lutheran theology student we learned at that time about the so-called corrections to the articles of Christian faith which were being prepared at the behest of the regime and were to be promulgated after the final victory. Horrible, blasphemous alterations, secretly planned behind the backs of the men who were undergoing indescribable suffering at the fighting fronts.

Equally secret were preparations for legislation re-

30

garding girls and women. It was planned that after the war women would be forced to make up for the frightful toll of lives by means of a systematic and shameless population policy. At a large student assembly Gauleiter Giessler had publicly announced to the women that it was better to "present the Führer with a child" than to hang on at the university.

The students had discovered a professor who, as one of them stated, was the best thing at the whole university. He was Professor Huber, Sophie's philosophy teacher. The medical students also attended his lectures, and one had to get there early to find a seat. The professor's lectures on Leibniz and his theodicy were excellent. Theodicy—the vindication of the justice of God, an important and complex area of philosophy—was of course particularly difficult in time of war. For how does one trace out the work of God in a world where killing and suffering are raging?

But when a teacher such as Huber presented the evidence, his interpretation became an unforgettable experience; it shed light on the present moment, when man was not only trampling on the divine order but also attempting to annihilate God himself. Before long, Hans had gotten to know Professor Huber, and at times the latter joined the group of students and carried on discussions with them. He was as intensely interested in all their problems as they were themselves. Though his hair was turning gray, he was one of them.

Sophie had been in Munich hardly six weeks when an incredible event occurred at the university. Leaflets were passing from hand to hand—leaflets produced on a duplicating machine. This occurrence caused intense excitement among the students. Feelings of triumph and enthusiasm, of disapproval and anger too, surged and swelled confusedly among the student body. Sophie secretly rejoiced when she heard the news. So it was true after all, something was abroad, and finally somebody had dared to act. Eagerly she seized one of the flyers and began to read. "The Leaflets of the White Rose" was the heading. "Nothing is so unworthy of a civilized people as allowing itself to be 'governed' without opposition by an irresponsible clique that has yielded to base instinct." She read on: "If everyone waits until the other man makes a start, the messengers of avenging Nemesis will come steadily closer; then even the last victim will have been cast senselessly into the maw of the insatiable demon. Therefore every individual conscious of his responsiblity as a member of Christian and Western civilization must defend himself as best he can at this late hour, he must work against the scourge of mankind, against fascism and any similar system of totalitarianism. Offer passive resistance—*resistance*—wherever you may be, forestall the spread of this atheistic war machine before it is too late, before the last cities, like Cologne, have been reduced to rubble, and before the nation's last young man has given his blood on some battlefield for the *hubris* of this subhuman. Do not forget that every people deserves the government it is willing to endure!"

To Sophie these words seemed strangely familiar, as if they were her own private thoughts. Suspicion arose within her and cold fear gripped her heart. What if Hans' words about the duplicating machine had been more than a casual remark? But no! Never!

When Sophie stepped from the university building into bright sunlight, her anxiety faded. How could she possibly have had this mad suspicion? All over Munich the populace was astir with rumors of secret rebellion.

A few minutes later she was in Hans' room, which smelled of jasmine and cigarettes. On the walls he had pinned up prints of modern French paintings. Sophie had not seen her brother on this day—he was probably on duty at the hospital. She decided to wait for him. She had put the leaflet out of her thoughts; while waiting she leafed idly through the books on the table. There! She saw a passage marked by a bookmark, a fine pencil line in the margin against it. It was one of those old-fashioned volumes of the classics, by Schiller; the opened page dealt with the ancient Greek lawgivers Lycurgus and Solon. She read: "Anything may be sacrificed to the good of the state except that end for which the state serves as means. The state is never an end in itself, it is important only as a condition under which the purposes of mankind can be attained, and this purpose is none other than the development of all of man's powers, his progress and improvement. If a state prevents the development of the capacities which reside in man, if it interferes with the progress of the human spirit, then it is reprehensible and injurious, no matter how excellently devised, how perfect in its own way." Where had she read these words? Had she not seen them this very day? In the leaflet! These words were printed there! For a long, painful moment she had the feeling of being another person. A strangling fear took hold of her, and a great, overwhelming remonstrance against Hans arose within her. Why he? Had he forgotten his father, the family at home who were in jeopardy as it was? Why did he not leave this job to people who were politically minded, people with experience and practical knowledge? Why did he not save himself for a great mission—he with his unusual talents? But the most terrifying thought of all was that he was now an outlaw. He had removed himself from the last zone of security into the realm of risk; he stood at the edge of existence, in that awesome place where inch by inch new ground is gained for mankind through struggle, heroic deeds, and suffering.

Sophie tried to master her fear. She tried to stop thinking about the leaflet. She put the resistance out of her mind and thought of her dearly beloved brother. He was adrift in a dangerous sea. Did she dare leave him now?

Could she sit here quietly and watch him go to his destruction? Was it not her duty to stand by him?

Oh, God, would it be possible to call a halt to this venture? Could she pull him back to the safe shore and preserve him for their parents, for himself, for the world and his life? Yet she knew that he had crossed the boundary within which people conduct their everyday lives in safety and comfort. There was no way back.

At last Hans arrived.

"Do you know where the leaflets come from?" Sophie asked.

"These days it's best not to know about certain things, so as not to endanger the lives of others."

"But, Hans, a man can't do a thing like this alone. The fact that nowadays only one person can be allowed to be in on a thing like this—surely that proves how irresistible this power is that can corrode the closest human ties and isolate us. By yourself your are powerless against them."

In the days that followed, there appeared at brief intervals three more of the leaflets of the White Rose. They also were found outside the university and in fact throughout the city, sporadically appearing in mailboxes. They were distributed in other southern German cities as well.

Then for a time no more appeared.

Among the students it was rumored that during the vacation the men were to be sent away for frontline service in Russia. Suddenly, just before the end of the semester, the rumor became reality. On a single day's notice they had to get ready for shipment to Russia.

The friends had gathered once more—it was the eve of the transport to the front. They held a farewell party. Professor Huber had come, and some other reliable students had been invited. Though the incident of the leaflets had

Kurt Huber, Munich, born October 24, 1893, professor of psychology and philosophy, executed July 13, 1943

occurred weeks before, it was still in the forefront of their thoughts. In the meantime other persons, just as cautiously as Sophie, had enlisted at Hans' side, sharing with him the knowledge and the heavy responsibility. On this last evening they wanted to survey and discuss the entire matter once more, and at the end of a serious review they came to a decision: should they be lucky enough to return from Russia, the Action of the White Rose would be fully developed and would form the bold beginning of a carefully coordinated, disciplined resistance movement. They agreed that the circle of members would have to be enlarged. Each man was to consider carefully which friends and acquaintances were reliable enough to be let in on the plan. Each of them would be assigned a small but important task, and Hans was to hold the reins of the whole undertaking.

"We will have to let the truth ring out as clearly and audibly as possible in the German night," said Professor Huber. "We must try to kindle the spark of resistance in the hearts of millions of honest Germans, so that it burns bright and bold. The isolated individuals who have stood up one by one against Hitler must be made aware that a large body of like-minded people stands with them. This knowledge will give them courage and the strength to persist. Beyond this, we must try to enlighten those Germans who are still unaware of the evil intentions of our government and awaken in them the will to resistance and forthright opposition. Perhaps we will succeed at the eleventh hour in shaking off the tyrannical oppressor and using that great moment for building, in concert with the other nations of Europe, a new and more humane world."

"And what if we don't succeed?" someone asked. "I doubt very much that we'll be able to storm these iron walls of fear and terror, which strangle every move toward rebellion at its inception."

"Then we must risk it anyway," answered Christl

36

with strong emotion. "Then it is our duty by our behavior and by our dedication to demonstrate that man's freedom still exists. Sooner or later the cause of humanity must be upheld, and then one day it will again prevail. We must gamble our 'No' against this power which has arrogantly placed itself above the essential human values and which is determined to root out all protest. We must do it for the sake of life itself—no one can absolve us of this responsibility. National Socialism is the name of a malignant spiritual disease that has befallen our people. We dare not remain silent as we watch its course, as the German people suffer its ravages."

They sat together late into the night. In discussions like this, in the pros and cons of opinion and doubt, they worked out the clear, firm understanding which was needed if they were to hold to their resolve. For it took a great deal of strength to swim against the current. But even more difficult and much more bitter was the need to hope for the defeat of one's own people, for that seemed to be the only possible way of ridding the country of the parasite draining the nation's strength.

Then the students left for the front, and for Sophie Munich became empty and unfamiliar. She packed her things and went home.

She had not been home long when her father received in the mail an indictment from the Special Court. A subsequent court hearing sentenced him to four months in prison.

Her father was in prison and her brothers and all her friends were at the Russian front, far away, out of reach.

It was very quiet at home but pleasant nonetheless, and Sophie enjoyed her stay. Home was like a ship sailing unperturbed and steady on the deep, strange waters of the times. It was like a ship—but sometimes it heaved and rocked, a tiny shell on the dark, murky, incalculable waves.

During a thunderstorm she had gone up to the roof with the little boy who was living with them and whom she loved dearly. She wanted to bring in the drying clothes before the rain came. At the sound of a loud clap of thunder the boy turned his face in fear toward hers. Then she showed him the lightning rod. After she had explained how it worked, he asked; "But does God understand about your lightning rod?"

"He knows about lightning rods and a great deal more; for if that were not so, then there wouldn't be one stone left standing on another in the world today. You need not fear."

Now and again nurses from Schwäbisch-Hall, former friends of her mother's, came to visit. In that city there was a large hospital for mentally ill children.

One day one of the nurses called. She was despondent and distraught, and we did not know how to help her. Finally she told us the reason for her grief. For some time past her wards had been carted off by the black vans of the SS and sent to their death in gas chambers. After the first contingents failed to return from their secret journey, a strange disturbance agitated the children in the institution. "Where are the trucks going, Auntie?"—"They are going to heaven," replied the nurses in their helplessness and confusion. From that time on, the children mounted the strange trucks singing.

A physician in one of the mental hospitals protested, "Over my dead body!" It is not known what became of him.

A soldier came home from Russia on furlough. He was the father of one of these children; he had never ceased hoping that the child would be cured. He felt toward his

38

son the love that only a father can feel. But when he arrived, the child was already dead.

By good fortune Hans had been sent to the front at a point close to his youngest brother. What a joy and surprise, deep in the Russian hinterlands, when unexpectedly Werner Scholl heard a familiar voice asking for him outside the bunker.

On a golden-blue day in late summer Hans received the news of his father's imprisonment. He took a horse and set out immediately to go to Werner. "I have a letter from home," said Hans as he handed it to his younger brother. Werner read it without a word. He peered into the distance, his eyes closed in a squint, but said nothing. At this moment Hans, in an unaccustomed gesture, placed his hand on the other's shoulder and said, "We mustn't take this blow as others would take it. It is a mark of distinction."

Slowly Hans rode back to his company. Out of the melancholy and the feeling of peace that filled his mind, memories arose.

During the transport to the front their train had stopped for a few minutes at a Polish station. Along the embankment he saw women and girls bent over and doing heavy men's work with picks. They wore the yellow Star of David on their blouses. Hans slipped through the window of his car and approached. The first one in the group was a young, emaciated girl with small, delicate hands and a beautiful, intelligent face that bore an expression of unspeakable sorrow. Did he have anything that he might give to her? He remembered his "Iron Ration"—a bar of chocolate, raisins, and nuts—and slipped it into her pocket. The girl threw it on the ground at his feet with a harassed but infinitely proud gesture. He picked it up, smiled, and said, "I wanted to do something to please you." Then he bent down, picked a daisy, and placed it and the package at her feet. The train was starting to move, and Hans had to take a couple of long leaps to get back on. From the window he could see that the girl was standing still, watching the departing train, the white flower in her hair.

Then he saw the eyes of an old Jewish man walking at the rear of a column of forced laborers. It was the finely modeled face of a scholar. Hans read there such an abyss of suffering as he had never before beheld. On impulse he took out his tobacco pouch and furtively pressed it in the old man's hand. Never would Hans forget the quick flash of joy which ignited in those eyes.

He remembered too that spring day in a first-aid station at home. One of the wounded men was to be discharged; the doctors had done a splendid job of patching him together. But just before his dismissal the wound suddenly and for no apparent reason began to bleed and could not be stopped. It lay close to the jugular vein of the neck, and there was but one thing to do: to find the vein and tie it. However, all efforts were useless; the man bled to death under the doctors' hands. Hans went out into the corridor, deeply shaken. At that moment he met the young wife of the man who had died. She had come to call for her husband: beautiful, radiant, blissful in her expectation, carrying a large bouquet of bright flowers.

When, when will the state finally recognize that it has no higher duty than to safeguard the happiness of the millions of ordinary people? When finally will the state forget about the ideals that ignore the needs of simple everyday life? And when will it understand that a small step, however difficult it may be, taken in the direction of peace for the individual, as for nations, is greater than victory in battle?

Hans' thoughts moved to his father in prison.

When Hans returned from Russia in the late autumn

40

of 1942 with his friends, his father was at liberty again.

The experiences at the front and in the army hospitals had made Hans and his friends maturer and manlier. These experiences had shown them more forcibly and more clearly than ever the need to oppose the regime with its terrible mania for annihilation. Out there the young men had seen how and on what an unimaginable scale human life was risked and wasted. If one's life is to be a gamble anyway, why not lose it in opposing the injustice that cried out to high heaven?

Now that they were back, they intended to take up the work in accordance with the decision they had made on the eve of their departure.

In a back lot not far from the apartment where my brother and sister lived there was a sort of garden house with a spacious studio. An artist who was on close terms with Hans' circle had given them the use of it when he was sent to the front; no one else lived in the little building. The group often met here now, and sometimes the students gathered at night and worked long hours in the basement at their duplicating machine. It was a test of patience to print thousands upon thousands of flyers. But a great sense of satisfaction also filled them as they worked—finally to be emerging from inactivity and passivity and to be busy. They undoubtedly passed many a happy night in this way. However, joy was clouded with anxiety almost beyond endurance. They realized with dismay how immeasurably lonely they were, that their closest friends would draw back from them in horror if they knew. For just to know what was going on entailed a tremendous danger. At these times they were fully aware that they walked a razor's edge. Who could know whether they were not already under surveillance; whether the neighbors to whom they innocently said hello had not already started the process that would lead to their capture; whether someone was not following them in the streets, observing all their movements; whether their fingerprints were not already on file? The solid ground of the city had become a crumbling tissue; would it be strong enough to hold them tomorrow? Each day that went by was a gift of life, and every night brought its concern about the morrow. Only sleep provided a merciful refuge. The yearning just for once to shake off these risks and dangers, to be free and unencumbered, seized them at times with great force. There were moments and hours when life simply seemed to be getting too difficult; when the uncertainties and the anxiety surged over them and engulfed their courage. Then there was no help but to descend deep within themselves, where a voice assured them that they were doing the right thing, that they would have to continue, even if they were all alone in the world. I believe that at such times the students were able to converse freely with God, with that Being whom they gropingly sought in their youth, whom they tried to find at the end point of all study, action, and work. At this time Christ became for them in a strange way the elder brother who was always there, closer even than death. He was their path which allowed of no return, the truth which gave answer to so many questions, and life itself, the whole of splendid life.

Another important task aside from the preparation of the leaflets was their distribution. They had to appear in the greatest possible number of cities, to be as effective as possible. Never before had the students engaged in any such activity. Everything had to be thought through, checked, and tested. What were the possible ways of getting the leaflets into the hands of the people? At what places, in what localities should they be left so that the greatest possible number of eyes would see them—but without leaving any trace of the originators? The students packed the leaflets in suitcases and rode with their dangerous cargo to

42

Alexander Schmorell, Munich, born September 16, 1917, medical student, executed July 13, 1943

the large cities of southern Germany—to Frankfurt, Stuttgart, Vienna; to Freiburg, Saarbrücken, Mannheim, Karlsruhe.

They had to stow their luggage in an inconspicuous place on the train; they had to get it past the numerous patrols of the army, the police, and even the Gestapo, who ran checks on the trains and sometimes inspected the luggage itself. And in the cities, where they arrived so often at night and were overtaken by air-raid alarms, they had to try to dispatch their business with skill and to good effect. What a victory if you completed a successful journey of this kind and were able to sleep on the return journey, relieved and free, the empty suitcase innocently above you in the luggage rack! And how anxious you were if someone as much as looked at you. What fright when anyone came toward you—and what relief when he passed by. Heart and head, mind and intelligence were continuously on guard to make sure that all means of covering your tracks had been employed. Day in, day out they lived with joy and the feeling of success, trouble and worry, doubt and risk.

More and more frequently newspapers ran brief notices of death sentences meted out by the People's Court to isolated individuals who had opposed the demonic tyrants of the people, even if only in their utterances. One day it was a well-known pianist, the next an engineer, a worker, or the head of a factory. Among them were priests, a student, or a high-ranking officer such as Udet,* who was cut down at the moment when his presence became em-

---

*Ernst Udet (1896–1941) was a famous ace of World War I who later served as head of the technical office in the air ministry, with the rank of general. He was reported a suicide on November 17, 1941, but it was widely believed that his death was arranged, since he had fallen out of favor because of his criticisms of the Hitler regime. The popular play by Carl Zuckmayer *Des Teufels General* (1946) was based on his career. — ARS

barassing. People disappeared without a trace, extinguished like candles in the wind, and whoever could not be removed in secret was given a state funeral. I still recall vividly the burial of Rommel. Though it was common knowledge that Hitler's henchmen had forced his suicide, everyone in Ulm who owned a brown uniform, from the youngest cub to the oldest SA member, was ordered to attend the ceremony. And I recall also how I dodged past the flags in a hurry to avoid having to salute.

The back pages of newspapers were filled with obituaries of fallen soldiers. With their peculiar iron crosses, these pages looked like cemeteries.

Only the front page had a different aspect. This was due to the large, almost unbearably heavy headlines: "Hate Is Our Prayer—And Victory Our Reward." Underneath the slogans, bold red lines looked like veins swollen in anger:

Hate is Our Prayer . . .
We Will March On, Though Everything Break into
    Fragments . . .

The papers were like mine fields. It was dangerous to go through them. The whole era, all Germany, was like a mine field—our poor, benighted fatherland.

The newspapers were laconic and noncommittal, and not only because of the paper shortage. It was their task to aid in the total quenching of the German intellect. They gave not so much as a hint about the village priest who was sent to prison because he had included in his Sunday prayers the name of a prisoner of war, serving at forced labor, who had been murdered. They made no mention of the fact that day after day not one but dozens of executions took place. God knows the newsreel cameras never got inside the prisons which were crowded to bursting, though the inmates resembled ghosts and skeletons rather than human bodies. They did not film the pale, drawn faces behind the bars; they did not record the pounding of hearts, the silent cry that went through all Germany.

The newsreels took no note of the young wife who, after an air raid, wandered about the streets of Dresden with a suitcase containing her dead child—the one thing she had left in all the world—looking for a cemetery where she could bury him.

They had nothing to say about the German soldier far away in Russia who was suddenly seized with horror when he saw a mother walking unafraid and with grim determination across no-man's land, tugging her dead child after her, and no one was able to persuade her to part with him.

The newspapers could not report the conversation which took place at a health resort between a friend of my father's and a prison chaplain who was recuperating from a nervous breakdown. Every day he had had to escort at least seven condemned men to the gallows.

The papers also failed to take notice of the ashen, utterly sorrowful face of the prisoner who, upon completion of his sentence, came to the gatehouse in happy expectation of picking up his discharge papers and his belongings but who was instead ordered shipped to a concentration camp.

Sometimes it seemed miraculous to us that spring returned to this land at all. Spring came and brought flowers to the empty, starving, rationed world. It brought hope, and the children in the streets played their age-old games. On a streetcar in Munich a couple of children sang innocently, unself-consciously, "Everything changes, everything passes—even Hitler and his masses."

The grown-ups, though—they hardly dared to laugh, though one knew what a sense of release this would have given them.

One evening Sophie waited for Hans. For some time now they had been living in a large two-room apartment. Their landlady was usually away in the country, since she was afraid of the bombers circling night after night above the city. Sophie had received a package from home with apples, butter, a large jar of marmalade, a huge coffee cake, and even some cookies. What wealth in a time of near starvation—their supper would be a feast! Sophie waited. She was happier than she had been for a long time She had set the table; the water for tea was boiling.

It grew dark—still no sign of Hans. Sophie's happy anticipation gave way to a mounting impatience. She would have liked to telephone his friends to find out where he was, but that was out of the question, for the Gestapo kept surveillance over the phones. Sophie went to her desk; at least she would try to do some sketching. It had been a long time since she had had an opportunity to work at her drawings. The previous summer with Alex had been the last time. But in this terrible time it was impossible to do more than keep up the struggle for existence. A manuscript lay on the desk, a fairytale they had made up when they were children and which her sister had now written down for her because Sophie had planned to prepare an illustrated children's book. But no, she was not able to draw; the waiting and worry eroded her imagination. Why didn't Hans come?

No matter where her thoughts turned, there was no way out. The whole world lay under a cloud of sadness. Would the sun ever come out again? She remembered her mother's face. At times she had seen on it the traces of pain around the eyes and mouth, an unnamable, indescribable record of suffering. Oh, God—so many thousands upon thousands of mothers with the same expression, eyes staring wide open to keep the tears from welling up . . . .

At that time Sophie wrote in her diary: "Many people

think that after our era the world will come to an end. The many terrible signs could make that belief plausible. But isn't this belief really only of incidental importance? For each of us, no matter in what age we live, have to be prepared at a moment's notice to be called to account by God. After all, do I know whether I'll be alive tomorrow morning? Tonight a bomb could wipe us all out. And then my guilt would not be any less than if I were to perish with the whole world and all the stars. I cannot understand why today "religious" people are worried about the existence of God just because men attack his works with sword and infamy. As if God didn't have the power (I feel that everything is in His hands)—the *power*. We must fear for the existence of mankind only because men turn away from Him who is their life."

In these weeks the Battle of Stalingrad reached its climax. Thousands of young men had been caught in the encirclement and driven into the merciless kettle of death, to perish of cold, starvation, and wounds. In her mind's eye Sophie saw the weary, harassed faces of people in crowded trains, bent over their pale sleeping children; people in flight from the Rhineland and the large cities of the north . . . . Bathing and sleep had been recommended by Thomas Aquinas as cures for melancholy. Sleep, yes, she wanted sleep—deep, dreamless sleep. When was the last time she had gotten a good night's rest?

She was awakened by a pleased, suppressed laugh and by steps in the hall. Finally Hans had returned. "We have a tremendous surprise for you. When you go down the Ludwigstrasse tomorrow, you'll pass signs saying 'Down With Hitler' about seventy times."

"And written in peacetime paint—they won't find it so easy to get it off," said Alex, as he entered, grinning, with Hans. Behind them was Willi. Without a word the latter set a bottle of wine on the table. Now the party

48

Willi Graf, born January 2, 1918, medical student, executed
October 12, 1943

could go on after all. And while the chilled young men warmed themselves, they told about that night's adventure.

The following morning Sophie left for the university a little earlier than usual. She took a roundabout way and walked down the length of the Ludwigstrasse. There the words were finally out in view: "Down With Hitler. Down With Hitler . . . ." When she got to the university she saw the word "Freedom" in the same paint over the entrance. Two women with brushes and sand were at work removing the slogan. "Let it stand," said Sophie. "That's meant to be read; that is why it was put there." The women looked at her and shook their heads: "No understand." They were Russians, sent to Germany for forced labor service.

While the enraged Nazis with great effort were clearing away the unexpected call for freedom from the Ludwig-strasse, the spark of rebellion had jumped to Berlin. A medical student who was a friend of Hans' had taken the responsibility of forming a resistance cell there and distributed copies of the leaflets drawn up in Munich.

In Freiburg, too, there were students who were spurred on by the courage of the Munich circle and who had decided to become active.

Later a girl student carried a leaflet to Hamburg, where another small group of students took up the task and spread the movement further.

In this way, according to the plans of Hans and his friends, one cell after another would come into being in the large cities, and from there the spirit of rebellion would spread in all directions.

They were still at work removing the traces of the street slogans. In the end, posters had to be pasted up to cover them. But Professor Huber was already at work drafting a new leaflet, this time to be addressed particularly to the students.

While he and Hans were wrestling with the wording of this flyer, into which they wanted to infuse all the sadness and outrage of an oppressed Germany, a round-about warning reached Hans that the Gestapo were on his track and that he must count on being arrested within a few days. Hans was inclined to shrug off this vague hint. Perhaps certain people who wished him well were trying to get him to stop his work. But it was the very obscurity and indefiniteness of the warning that plunged him into doubt.

Ought he not to put this whole difficult way of life in Germany, with its constant threat of danger, behind him and flee to a free country, to Switzerland? It should not be any problem for him, a mountain climber and seasoned sportsman, to slip across the border illegally. He had lived through plenty of situations at the front where cool self-control and presence of mind had saved him.

But in that case what would happen to his friends and his family? His flight would bring them under immediate suspicion, while he would be watching from free Switzerland as they were haled before the People's Court and sent to concentration camps. He could never endure that. A hundred threads tied him to this place, and the devilish system was so ingeniously devised that he would endanger the lives of a hundred people if he placed himself in safety. He alone had to take the responsibility. He had to stay, so as to keep the circle of harm as small as possible; and if the storm should break over his head, he must take all blame upon himself.

In the days following, Hans worked with redoubled energy. He spent night after night with his friends and Sophie in the cellar of the studio at the duplicating machine. The nation's dejection and shock resulting from Stalingrad must not again be engulfed by the gray, indifferent routine of everyday life. Before that happened, he wanted to show that not all Germans were of a mind to accept this murderous war without a murmur.

On a sunny Thursday—it was February 18, 1943—the work had progressed so far that, before going to the university, Hans and Sophie were able to pack a suitcase with leaflets. Both were pleased and in good spirits as they made their way toward the university with the handbag, though in the night Sophie had had a dream which she could not shake loose, in which the Gestapo had come and arrested the two of them.

Hardly had brother and sister left the house when a friend rang the bell, his mission being to bring them an urgent warning. But since he was unable to find out where they had gone, he waited. Probably everything that happened later was the result of their failure to receive this message.

In the meantime they had arrived at the university, and since the lecture rooms were to open in a few minutes, they quickly decided to deposit the leaflets in the corridors. Then they disposed of the remainder by letting the sheets fall from the top level of the staircase down into the entrance hall. Relieved, they were about to go, but a pair of eyes had spotted them. It was as if these eyes—(they belonged to the building superintendent)—had been detached from the being of their owner and turned into automatic spyglasses of the dictatorship. The doors of the building were immediately locked, and the fate of brother and sister was sealed.

The Gestapo, who had been speedily notified, carried them off to their prison, the infamous Wittelsbach Palace. And now the interrogations started, day and night, hour after hour. They were out of communication with the world, out of touch with their friends; they were not even told whether any of their associates had been apprehended. Sophie learned from a fellow prisoner that Christl Probst had been "delivered" a few hours after them. For the first time her self-control was shaken, and wild despair threatened to overpower her—Christl, the same Christl whom they had hoped to spare because he was the father of three small children. And Herta, his wife, was still lying in after the birth of the youngest child. Sophie saw Christl standing before her, as he had been on a bright September day when she and Hans had visited his family in the little house in the mountains of upper Bavaria. Christl was holding his two-year-old boy in his arms and looking with fascination into the peaceful face of his child. His delicate, courageous young wife could hardly feel secure in her own four walls; some years earlier her two brothers had had to flee from the Gestapo and no one knew whether they were still alive. But if there was as much as a spark of justice in this state, Sophie reflected in her despair, then nothing should, nothing must happen to Christl.

All who in those days were in contact with them— their fellow prisoners, the chaplains, the guards, and even the Gestapo officials—were deeply impressed by their bravery and the dignity of their bearing. Like a ray of bright light their cheerful composure and calm stood in marked contrast to the hectic tensions of the Gestapo headquarters. Their action had occasioned great consternation at all levels in the upper echelons of the Party and the government. A secret triumph of helpless decency, of fettered freedom, over brutality and lawlessness seemed to be happening, and the news of it blew like an early spring breeze through prisons and concentration camps. Many persons who encountered Hans and Sophie in prison told us about their last days and hours.

These fragmentary reports came together like tiny magnets to form a pattern, a picture of several days of strenuous life. It was as if in these days their many unlived years were compacted into a heightened level of activity.

I had had the opportunity after their death, in the endless dragging hours of uncertainty and pain while in prison, to think about the behavior, the words, and the task of my sister and brother and their friends, and I tried despite the pain of my bereavement to understand the underlying political significance of their acts.

After the second day of their detention it became clear that they must expect a sentence of death. They came to terms with this knowledge in a clear-headed way. At first, until their efforts to hold back information had become meaningless in the face of the evidence and proof of their complicity, they had conceived and chosen a different course: to survive and to take their part in the creation of a new order after the rule of force was overthrown. Just a few weeks earlier Hans had announced a decision—taken perhaps in the light of the numerous death sentences then being handed out: "This must be avoided under any circumstances. We must live, so that afterward we'll be there; they will need us. Prison and concentration camp—yes, if need be. One can survive that; but we mustn't put our lives in jeopardy."

But now the situation had suddenly changed; now there was no way out. Only one way was left: circumspectly and calmly to make sure that the smallest number of others would be drawn in; to make it perfectly evident by one's bearing what it was that one wanted to defend and hold high; to be independent and free, to bear the stamp of a strong spirit.

All three were determined (though they had no communication with one another) to take upon themselves the so-called blame for everything, in order to lighten the burden of the others. The Gestapo officials rubbed their hands in glee over the abundant flow of confessions. Brother and sister searched their memories to identify the "crimes" which could be laid at their door. It was like a great trial of strength for the life of their friends, and after every successful interrogation they returned to their cells with a sense of achievement.

Thus they must have experienced those days as an existence beyond the realm of the living but at the same time freed from death—still deeply involved with the concerns of life. The measures taken by the police to prevent their suicide must have struck them as ridiculous and in bad taste. No blade, no object was permitted in the cell; they were not even permitted their privacy; a fellow prisoner was at all times placed close by, to make sure that they would not try to forestall the executioner. Day and night the lights were kept burning in their cells.

These were difficult hours, especially for Hans. Would the interrogations proceed in the right way? Would he always have the presence of mind to give the right answer, so that no name, no hint, no suspicious statement would slip out? With alert, intelligent interest they submitted to the examinations. According to the reports of his fellow prisoners, Hans was able to display a relaxed cheerfulness in the short intervals between interrogations. But then there followed difficult hours of concern for his friends, of pain at causing his family a leavetaking of this kind.

Finally the last morning arrived. Hans requested his cellmate to take note of a number of matters that were to be reported to his parents and friends. Then he shook hands, in a kindly and almost ceremonious way: "Let's say good-bye now, while we are still by ourselves." He silently turned and wrote some words on the white prison wall. For a moment it was quiet in the cell. Hardly had he laid the pencil aside when the keys rattled and the guards came, handcuffed him, and led him before the assembled court. The words on the wall remained—words by Goethe, which his father had often repeated to himself as he paced up and down in meditation and whose pathos had once brought a smile to Hans' lips: "Hold out in defiance of all despotism."

The students had no opportunity to select a defense lawyer. To be sure, the court named a lawyer as a matter of routine, but he was little more than a helpless puppet. Neither Sophie nor the others expected the slightest assistance from him. "If my brother is sentenced to die, you mustn't let them give me a lighter sentence, for I am exactly as guilty as he," she told him calmly. With all her power of concentration and thought she was with her brother in those days, and she was greatly concerned for his welfare because she surmised that he labored under a great burden. She asked the lawyer whether Hans as a soldier with service at the front had the right to execution by firing squad. To this question she was given an ambiguous reply. The lawyer was absolutely horrified at her next question—whether she would be publicly hanged or would be executed on the guillotine. He was not prepared for that sort of question, especially from a girl.

During these last nights, when she was not being interrogated, Sophie enjoyed the sound sleep of a child. Only once, at the moment when they handed her the indictment, was she shaken. After she had read the charges, she breathed easily again. "God be thanked," was all that she said.

Then she stretched out on the cot and began to meditate aloud about her death. "Such a fine, sunny day—and I have to go. But how many are dying on the battlefield in these days, how many young promising lives .... What does my death matter if through us thousands of people will be stirred to action and awakened?" It is a Sunday, and outside the prison, crowds of people are walking by the fence, all unsuspecting, enjoying the early spring sun.

When Sophie was awakened after her last night, while still seated on the cot she told of her dream: "It was a sunny day. I was carrying a child in a long white dress to

56

At the Munich railway station, summer 1942: Hans Scholl (left), Sophie Scholl (behind the fence), Alexander Schmorell (right), Willi Graf (back to camera); the other figure is unidentified.   *Photo: Jürgen Wittenstein*

be baptized. The way to the church led up a steep slope, but I held the child in my arms firmly and without faltering. Then suddenly the footing gave way and there was a great crevice in a glacier. I had just time enough to set the child down on the other side before plunging into the abyss."

She tried to explain the meaning of this simple dream to her fellow prisoners. "The child is our idea. In spite of all obstacles, it will prevail. We were permitted to be pioneers, though we must die early for its sake."

After a short while her cell, too, was empty. She left the indictment sheet behind, and on its reverse we found the word "Freedom" hastily scribbled.

My parents had received word of the arrests on Friday, the day after the event, first from a friend, a woman student, then later by a phone call from an unidentified student whose message sounded sorrowful and despairing. They decided at once to visit the prisoners and to do everything possible to lighten their burden.

But what could they do in their helplessness? In a time like this, a time of great trouble, faced with an immediate decision, one's impulse is to rush in and try to batter down walls. Since the weekend intervened, when no visits were permitted, they waited until Monday to travel by train with my youngest brother, Werner (unexpectedly returned two days before on leave from Russia). There on the platform, waiting in great agitation, was the student who had called them about the arrest, and he said, "We have very little time. The People's Court is in session, and the hearing is already under way. We must prepare ourselves for the worst." No one had expected such haste, and only later did we learn that summary proceedings had been instituted, because the judges wanted to arrange a speedy and frightening execution as a warning to others.

My mother bravely asked, "Will they have to die?" The student nodded in desperation, obviously very upset. "If I had just one tank," he cried out in helpless anguish, "and a handful of people, I might still be able to rescue them. I would break up the court session and carry them to the border." They hurried to the Palace of Justice and forced their way into the chamber where invited Nazi guests had been seated. There sat the judges in their red robes, Freisler* in the center, all fuming and sputtering in rage.

Calm and upright in their seats, and very much alone, the three young defendants sat opposite. They gave their replies openly and deliberately. Sophie said at one point (though she spoke very, very little), "What we said and wrote is what many people are thinking. Only they don't dare to say it." The attitude and bearing of the three was of such dignity that they drew even the hostile part of the audience under their spell.

By the time my parents managed to push their way in, the trial was nearly over. They arrived just in time to hear the sentences pronounced. My mother lost her strength for a moment and had to be escorted out of the room. A wave of excitement went through the room when my father cried out, "There is a higher court before which we all must stand!" My mother quickly regained her composure, and afterward all her thoughts and plans were fixed on drawing up a petition for mercy and meeting her children. She was marvelously self-possessed, clear in her mind and brave, a comfort to all the others who otherwise would have been called upon to help her. After the trial my youngest brother pushed his way down to the prisoners

---

*Roland Freisler, notorious Nazi judge and President of the People's Court, presided at the trial. — ARS

and took their hands. With tears welling in his eyes, Hans calmly laid his hand on his shoulder. "Be strong. Admit nothing." Yes, concede nothing, either in life or at the point of death. They had not tried to save themselves by pretending to hold orthodox National Socialist views, by citing their good record, or by anything of that kind. Anyone who has been present at one of these political trials in the era of the Third Reich knows what that meant. In the face of death or prison (and one cannot blame those who tried to save themselves), face to face with these devilish judges, many persons tried to conceal their true opinions so as to safeguard their lives and their future.

Each of the three was called upon in the customary way to make a statement at the close of the trial. Sophie said nothing. Christl requested that his life be spared for the sake of his children. Hans supported Christl's plea and put in a word for his friend. But Freisler brutally cut him off. "If you have nothing to say on your own behalf, please be quiet."

Words can probably never do justice to the hours that followed.

The three were transferred to the large execution jail at München-Stadelheim, situated close by the cemetery at the edge of the Perlach Forest.

There they wrote their farewell letters. Sophie requested that she be permitted an interview with the Gestapo investigator, since she wanted to make a supplementary statement. She had recalled something that might exonerate one of the other two.

Christl, who had been reared outside the Church, asked to see a priest. He wanted to be baptized, having inwardly long since accepted the Roman Catholic faith. In a letter to his mother he wrote, "I thank you for the gift of life. If I consider matters properly now, it was nothing other than the road to God. I am preceding you by a little, to prepare you a splendid reception."

Meanwhile my parents had the miraculous good fortune of being able to visit their children once more. It was almost impossible to obtain such permission. Between four and five o'clock they hurried to the prison. They still did not know that their children's last hour was so near.

First Hans was brought out. He wore a prison uniform, he walked upright and briskly, and he allowed nothing in the circumstances to becloud his spirit. His face was thin and drawn, as if after a difficult struggle, but now it beamed radiantly. He bent lovingly over the barrier and took his parents' hands. "I have no hatred. I have put everything, everything behind me." My father embraced him and said, "You will go down in history—there is such a thing as justice in spite of all this." Then Hans asked them to take his greetings to all his friends. When at the end he mentioned one further name, a tear ran down his face; he bent low so that no one would see. And then he went out, without the slightest show of fear, borne along by a profound inner strength.

Then Sophie was brought in by a woman warden. She wore her regular clothes and walked slowly, relaxedly, and very upright. (Nowhere does one learn to bear oneself so proudly as in prison.) Her face bore a smile like that of a person looking into the sun. Willingly and cheerfully she accepted the candy that Hans had refused: "Oh yes, of course, I didn't have any lunch." It was an indescribable affirmation of life to the end, to the very last moment. She too was noticeably thinner, but her face revealed a marvelous sense of triumph. Her skin was rosy and fresh—this struck her mother as never before—and her lips were a glowing deep red. "So now you will never again set foot in our house," said Mother. "Oh, what do these few short years matter, Mother," she answered. Then she remarked, as had Hans, firmly, with conviction, and in triumph, "We took all the blame, for everything." And she added, "That is bound to have its effect in time to come."

Sophie had been chiefly concerned in those days whether her mother would be able to bear the ordeal of losing two children at the same moment. But now, as Mother stood there, so brave and good, Sophie had a feeling of sudden release from anxiety. Again her mother spoke; she wanted to give her daughter something she might hold fast to: "You know, Sophie—Jesus." Earnestly, firmly, almost imperiously Sophie replied, "Yes, but you too." Then she left—free, fearless, and calm. She was still smiling.

Christl was not able to see any of his family. His wife was not yet out of the hospital after the birth of their third child. She did not learn of her husband's fate until after the execution.

The prison guards reported: "They bore themselves with marvelous bravery. The whole prison was impressed by them. That is why we risked bringing the three of them together once more—at the last moment before the execution. If our action had become known, the consequences for us would have been serious. We wanted to let them have a cigarette together before the end. It was just a few minutes that they had, but I believe that it meant a great deal to them. 'I didn't know that dying can be so easy,' said Christl Probst, adding, 'In a few minutes we will meet in eternity.'

"Then they were led off, the girl first. She went without the flicker of an eyelash. None of us understood how this was possible. The executioner said he had never seen anyone meet his end as she did."

And Hans, before he placed his head on the block— Hans called out so that the words rang through the huge prison: "Long live freedom!"

At first it seemed as if the matter was ended with the death of these three. They disappeared silently and in virtual secrecy into the earth of the Perlach cemetery, just as the bright sun of late winter was setting. "Greater love hath no man than this, that a man lay down his life for his friends," said the prison chaplain, who revealed himself as one of them and who ministered to them with complete understanding. He shook their hands and pointed to the setting sun, saying, "It will rise again."

But after a short time there followed one arrest after another, and in a second trial—we learned of it on Good Friday, while in prison—three further death sentences (together with a number of prison sentences) were issued by the People's Court to Professor Huber, Willi Graf, and Alexander Schmorell.

The posthumous papers of Professor Huber, who continued tirelessly to work at his studies in detention, both before and after sentencing, contained the following draft of a "Final Statement of the Accused." It has been reported that these remarks—or at least their essence—were delivered before the court:

> As a German citizen, as a German professor, and as a political person, I hold it to be not only my right but also my moral duty to take part in the shaping of our German destiny, to expose and oppose obvious wrongs. . . .
>
> What I intended to accomplish was to rouse the student body, not by means of an organization, but solely by my simple words; to urge them, not to violence, but to moral insight into the existing serious deficiencies of our political system. To urge the return to clear moral principles, to the constitutional state, to mutual trust between men. That is not illegal; rather, it is the restitution of legality. I asked myself, following

Kant's categorical imperative, what would happen if these subjective maxims governing my actions were to become universal law. To this there can be but one answer: public order, security, trust in the government and in our political life would be restored. Every morally responsible person would raise his voice in concert with ours against the threatening rule of raw force over justice, against mere arbitrariness over the will to the moral good. The demand of free self-determination of even the smallest national minority has been abused throughout Europe, and no less the requirement that racial and national identity be safeguarded. The basic right of true community of peoples has been abrogated by the systematic undermining of trust among men. There is no more terrible judgment of a community of peoples than the admission, which we all must make, that not one of us any longer feels safe from his neighbors, no father from his own sons.

It was this that I intended, that I had to do.

For all external legality there is an ultimate limit, beyond which it becomes untrue and immoral. This point is reached when it is used as a cloak for cowardice which will not stand up against open injustice. A state which suppresses free expression of opinion and which subjects to terrible punishment every—yes, any and all—morally justified criticism and all proposals for improvement by characterizing them as "Preparation for High Treason" breaks an unwritten law, a law which has always lived in the sound instincts of the people and which will always have to remain alive.

His statement must have ended more or less like this:

I have achieved the goal of uttering this warning and word of caution, not in a small, private gathering, but

64

before a responsible authority, the highest judiciary in the land. In order to give this admonition, this earnest plea for a return to right principles, I have pledged my life. I demand the return of freedom for our German people. We do not want to waste our short life enslaved and in chains, though they be the golden chains of material abundance and prosperity.

You have stripped from me the rank and privileges of the professorship and the doctoral degree summa cum laude which I earned, and you have set me at the level of the lowest criminal. The inner dignity of the university teacher, of the frank, courageous protestor of his philosophical and political views—no trial for treason can rob me of that. My actions and my intentions will be justified in the inevitable course of history; such is my firm faith. I hope to God that the inner strength that will vindicate my deeds will in good time spring forth from my own people. I have done as I had to do on the prompting of an inner voice. I take the consequences upon myself in the way expressed in the beautiful words of Johann Gottlieb Fichte:

> And thou shalt act as if
> On thee and on thy deed
> Depended the fate of all Germany,
> And thou alone must answer for it."

At that time it was rumored that about eighty people from Munich and other cities of southern and western Germany were subsequently apprehended. Some of these were relatives of the principals (usually quite unaware of what had been going on), who were taken into "kinship custody." "Kin must be held responsible for the traitor," was the order of the authorities, who were endeavoring to stamp out at the root any impulse toward independent

65

political action.

At the second trial, held on April 19, 1943, in which Professor Kurt Huber, Willi Graf, and Alexander Schmorell were sentenced to death, an additional eleven defendants were brought to the court. Three secondary school students —Hans Hirzel, Heinrich Guter, and Franz Müller—received jail sentences of up to five years. The university students Traute Lafrenz, Gisela Schertling, Käte Schüddekopf, and Susanne Hirzel—all members of the group to which my brother and sister had belonged—were each sentenced to a year in jail. Severe prison sentences of up to life were imposed on Eugen Grimminger, the medical student Helmut Bauer, and Dr. Heinrich Bollinger. Grimminger was an economic adviser in Stuttgart and had long been a friend of my father's. Day in and day out he had devotedly engaged in passive resistance, helping the oppressed and persecuted and giving financial support to the Munich action. His wife, Jenny, was murdered in the Auschwitz concentration camp on December 2, 1943. Bauer and Bollinger belonged to the group of friends headed by Willi Graf which for years had been strongly opposed to National Socialism; it is known that Bollinger was preparing for overt opposition by assembling a small stock of weapons.

It was characteristic that hardly a word appeared in the public print about these important and stirring trials. A spare notice of about thirty lines in the *Völkischer Beobachter*, under the headline "Just Punishment for Traitors to the Nation at War," was intended to minimize the affair. Nevertheless, the news about the events in Munich spread like wildfire even as far as the Russian front. It went like a wave of relief through concentration camps, prisons, and ghettos. At last a few individuals had expressed the sentiments that weighed so heavily on the hearts of millions. What another man of the resistance, Helmuth von Moltke, later demanded—"Make us into a legend!"—had

Hans Scholl, Sophie Scholl, Christoph Probst, summer 1942

Photo: Jürgen Wittenstein

come about in a few weeks; not in the same way, of course, as in a world where press and television bring immediate and repeated reports, but perhaps to even more intense effect. The underground exists by laws of its own.

On July 13, 1943 (strangely enough, on the same day as the execution of Professor Huber and Alexander Schmorell) a third trial growing out of the action of the Munich students took place. Four older friends of the group were brought before a special court: the bookseller Josef Söhngen, who had had a part in the editing of the leaflets; Harald Dohrn, Christoph Probst's father-in-law; the artist Wilhelm Geyer; and the architect-painter Manfred Eickemayer, who had turned over his studio for meetings and their work. Each of these was sentenced to three months in jail.

Harald Dohrn and his brother-in-law Hans Quecke later gave up their lives for the cause—the last of the Munich group to do so. During the "Freedom Campaign" of the last weeks of the war in the spring of 1945, which was under the leadership of the lawyer Dr. Gerngross and which had proclaimed the occupation of the Munich radio station by the resistance, these two men had come forward to offer their services. Through a combination of tragic circumstances they were discovered and shot to death by the SS in a forest near Munich. They lie buried only a few hundred yards from the graves of the first victims, Sophie and Hans Scholl and Christoph Probst.

During the autumn of 1942, but more especially in spring and summer 1943, a second complex of the resistance was disclosed and subsequently entered the history of German resistance under the name of the "Hamburg Branch of the White Rose." As in Munich, it was made up of a group of students and intellectuals, and it embraced about fifty persons, of whom, according to the documents of the Gestapo and the People's Court, 32 were imprisoned in concentration camps or in prisons in the fall of 1943. In a report by Ilse Jacob, the group is described as follows:

The Hamburg group of the White Rose had come into being under the influence of the first Munich leaflets. Not all the individual members were acquainted with one another, and in some cases they did not meet until they were in prison or in a concentration camp. The efforts made to coordinate the work of the several circles within the group were undertaken primarily by Albert Suhr and Heinz Kucharski who, for example, planned to set up a radio transmitter. The members met regularly in two Hamburg bookstores for evening discussions.

In the Hamburg group there were some seventeen-year-olds who were still attending school or who had been inducted into the Labor Service or the War Aide Service. They had been educated in National Socialist schools and youth organizations. Their resistance started, as one of them wrote, over a clash of opinion. Following their bent and interests, they thought and did what in Cambridge or Basel would have been the most natural thing in the world. But in Germany these matters became a "conflict involving high political matters," or "high treason zealously prosecuted by the Gestapo and the People's Court."

Communication between the Munich and the Hamburg groups was effected by the medical student Traute Lafrenz of Hamburg, who had studied in Munich since 1941 and who was a close friend of Alexander Schmorell and Hans and Sophie Scholl. In the fall of 1942 she delivered the Munich Leaflets of the White Rose of the preceding summer to her Hamburg comrades, Greta Rothe, Heinz Kucharski, and Karl Ludwig Schneider. Shortly after the

Munich group was eliminated by the trials of February, April, and June, 1943—in the course of which Traute Lafrenz was also imprisoned—Hans Leipelt, a student of chemistry, saw to it that the Leaflets of the White Rose continued to be distributed. In addition, he organized a movement expressing solidarity and support for the impoverished widow of Professor Huber and their two children, whose pension had been withdrawn by the National Socialist state.

Hans Leipelt had moved from Hamburg to Munich as early as the winter of 1941 in order to continue his studies in chemistry. The Chemical Institute of Munich University, under the direction of Professor Heinrich Wieland, was known as a refuge for opponents and victims of the regime. Again and again this noble and fearless scientist, in contravention of the National Socialist race laws, took "non-Aryan" students into the institute and thus saved them from forced labor or worse.

As far as is known, Leipelt had no direct contact with my brother Hans and sister Sophie, but did know some of their friends in Munich. He can be considered the central link between the Hamburg and the Munich student resistance after the Gestapo seized Traute Lafrenz . In Hamburg, too, the leaflets were distributed, and collections were taken up for Frau Clara Huber. Neither Leipelt and his circle in Munich, nor the Hamburg group, including his friends Heinz Kucharski, Albert Suhr, Karl-Ludwig Schneider and Bruno Himpkamp, were paralyzed by the series of death sentences already carried out.

A year after the arrest of Leipelt, on October 13, 1944, the fourth court trial of the White Rose took place. This time Hans Leipelt was sentenced to death, and three of his seven co-defendants received long prison terms. Leipelt was brought to the execution jail of München-Stadelheim, where he was executed on the guillotine on January 29,

1945. In Hamburg a total of four additional court trials took place on April 17, 19, and 20, 1945: the cases *Kucharski et al.*, *Suhr et al.*, *Schneider et al.*, and *Himpkamp et al.* Most of the imprisoned defendants had already been freed by U. S. Forces in the cities of Stendal and Bayreuth. In Hamburg, however, where Heinz Kucharski, Dr. Rudolph Degkwitz, Felix Jud, Thorsten Müller, and Ilse Ledien were still imprisoned, the People's Court sentenced Heinz Kucharski to death on April 17, 1945; they imposed a year's sentence on Dr. Rudolph Degkwitz; and, on April 19, 1945, the bookseller Felix Jud was sentenced to four years' imprisonment.

It was fortunate for the Hamburg group that the trials were so prolonged, since this circumstance prevented other persons from being drawn into the whirlpool. In this regard, too, the Allies closed the Nazi accounts. Kucharski was to make a hair's breadth escape from his executioners on the way to the guillotine at Bützow-Dreibergen. The list of the dead of the Hamburg branch of the White Rose contains the names of:

Katharina Leipelt, mother of Hans, Doctor of Science, born May 28, 1893, forced to take her life on January 9, 1944

Elisabeth Lange, born July 7, 1900, forced to take her life on January 28, 1944

Reinhold Meyer, student of philosophy, born July 18, 1920, died on November 12, 1944, in prison at Fuhlsbüttel

Hans Leipelt, student of science, born July 18, 1920, beheaded on January 29, 1945

Frederick Geussenhainer, candidate for a medical degree, born April 24, 1912, died in April 1945 in the concentration camp at Mauthausen

Greta Rothe, candidate for a medical degree, born

June 13, 1919, died on April 15, 1945 in the prison
of Leipzig-Meusdorf

Curt Ledien, Doctor of Laws, born June 5, 1893,
hanged on April 23, 1945

Gretl Mrosek, born December 14, 1915, hanged on
April 21, 1945

In the first months of 1945 the world waited in suspense
for the imminent end of the war and thus of the Nazi regime.
Within all the prisoners and condemned men there burned
the flickering hope that they might still win out in the race
against time. On the other hand, the risks and dangers
were also steadily becoming more acute, for the glimpse
of their own downfall caused the Nazi rulers to be all the
more severe. Their revenge against people who as individuals had dared to attack the essential idea of the regime
was to pull their opponents down to death along with themselves.

Leaflets of the White Rose*

Nothing is so unworthy of a civilized nation as allowing itself to be "governed" without opposition by an irresponsible clique that has yielded to base instinct. It is certain that today every honest German is ashamed of his government. Who among us has any conception of the dimensions of shame that will befall us and our children when one day the veil has fallen from our eyes and the most horrible of crimes—crimes that infinitely outdistance every human measure—reach the light of day? If the German people are already so corrupted and spiritually crushed that they do not raise a hand, frivolously trusting in a questionable faith in lawful order in history; if they surrender man's highest principle, that which raises him above all other God's creatures, his free will; if they abandon the will to take

---

*There were four leaflets in the series "Leaflets of the White Rose." The first of these was prepared in the summer or fall of 1942, and all were issued before the Allied landings in Morocco and Algeria, November 8, 1942.

The series headed "Leaflets of the Resistance" was begun in 1943, and the Munich group had prepared only two of these before they were apprehended. Of these two "A Call to All Germans" was written before the defeat at Stalingrad (January 31, 1943), and the second, "Fellow Fighters in the Resistance!" came out after Stalingrad and at most a day or two before the Scholls were seized by the Gestapo on February 18. The last leaflet was variously headed "Fellow Fighters in the Resistance!" ("Kommilitonen! Kommilitoninnen!") and "German Students!" ("Deutsche Studenten!").

decisive action and turn the wheel of history and thus subject it to their own rational decision; if they are so devoid of all individuality, have already gone so far along the road toward turning into a spiritless and cowardly mass—then, yes, they deserve their downfall. Goethe speaks of the Germans as a tragic people, like the Jews and the Greeks, but today it would appear rather that they are a spineless, will-less herd of hangers-on, who now—the marrow sucked out of their bones, robbed of their center of stability—are waiting to be hounded to their destruction. So it seems—but it is not so. Rather, by means of gradual, treacherous, systematic abuse, the system has put every man into a spiritual prison. Only now, finding himself lying in fetters, has he become aware of his fate. Only a few recognized the threat of ruin, and the reward for their heroic warning was death. We will have more to say about the fate of these persons. If everyone waits until the other man makes a start, the messengers of avenging Nemesis will come steadily closer; then even the last victim will have been cast senselessly into the maw of the insatiable demon. Therefore every individual, conscious of his responsibility as a member of Christian and Western civilization, must defend himself as best he can at this late hour, he must work against the scourges of mankind, against fascism and any similar system of totalitarianism. Offer passive resistance—*resistance*—wherever you may be, forestall the spread of this atheistic war machine before it is too late, before the last cities, like Cologne, have been reduced to rubble, and before the nation's last young man has given his blood on some battlefield for the *hubris* of a sub-human. Do not forget that every people deserves the regime it is willing to endure."

From Friedrich Schiller's "The Lawgiving of Lycurgus and Solon":

Viewed in relation to its purposes, the law code of

Lycurgus is a masterpiece of political science and knowledge of human nature. He desired a powerful, unassailable state, firmly established on its own principles. Political effectiveness and permanence were the goal toward which he strove, and he attained this goal to the full extent possible under the circumstances. But if one compares the purpose Lycurgus had in view with the purposes of mankind, then a deep abhorrence takes the place of the approbation which we felt at first glance. Anything may be sacrificed to the good of the state except that end for which the State serves as a means. The state is never an end in itself; it is important only as a condition under which the purpose of mankind can be attained, and this purpose is none other than the development of all of man's powers, his progress and improvement. If a state prevents the development of the capacities which reside in man, if it interferes with the progress of the human spirit, then it is reprehensible and injurious, no matter how excellently devised, how perfect in its own way. Its very permanence in that case amounts more to a reproach than to a basis for fame; it becomes a prolonged evil, and the longer it endures, the more harmful it is. . . .

At the price of all moral feeling a political system was set up, and the resources of the state were mobilized to that end. In Sparta there was no conjugal love, no mother love, no filial devotion, no friendship; all men were citizens only, and all virtue was civic virtue.

A law of the state made it the duty of Spartans to be inhumane to their slaves; in these unhappy victims of war humanity itself was insulted and mistreated. In the Spartan code of law the dangerous principle was promulgated that men are to be looked upon as means and not as ends—and the foundations of natural law and of morality were destroyed by that law. . . .

What an admirable sight is afforded, by contrast, by the rough soldier Gaius Marcius in his camp before Rome, when he renounced vengeance and victory because he could not endure to see a mother's tears! . . .

The state [of Lycurgus] could endure only under the one condition: that the spirit of the people remained quiescent. Hence it could be maintained only if it failed to achieve the highest, the sole purpose of a state.

From Goethe's *The Awakening of Epimenides*, Act II, Scene 4.

SPIRITS:
Though he who has boldly risen from the abyss
Through an iron will and cunning
May conquer half the world,
Yet to the abyss he must return.
Already a terrible fear has seized him;
In vain he will resist!
And all who still stand with him
Must perish in his fall.

HOPE:
Now I find my good men
Are gathered in the night,
To wait in silence, not to sleep.
And the glorious word of liberty
They whisper and murmur,
Till in unaccustomed strangeness,
On the steps of our temple
Once again in delight they cry:

Freedom! Freedom!

Please make as many copies of this leaflet as you can and distribute them.

It is impossible to engage in intellectual discourse with National Socialism because it is not an intellectually defensible program. It is false to speak of a National Socialist philosophy, for if there were such an entity, one would have to try by means of analysis and discussion either to prove its validity or to combat it. In actuality, however, we face a totally different situation. At its very inception this movement depended on the deception and betrayal of one's fellow man; even at that time it was inwardly corrupt and could support itself only by constant lies. After all, Hitler states in an early edition of "his" book (a book written in the worst German I have ever read, in spite of the fact that it has been elevated to the position of the Bible in this nation of poets and thinkers): "It is unbelievable, to what extent one must betray a people in order to rule it." If at the start this cancerous growth in the nation was not particularly noticeable, it was only because there were still enough forces at work that operated for the good, so that it was kept under control. As it grew larger, however, and finally in an ultimate spurt of growth attained ruling power, the tumor broke open, as it were, and infected the whole body. The greater part of its former opponents went into hiding. The German intellectuals fled to their cellars, there, like plants struggling in the dark, away from light and sun, gradually to choke to death. Now the end is at hand. Now it is our task to find one another again, to spread information from person to person, to keep a steady purpose, and to allow ourselves no rest until the last man is persuaded of the urgent need of his struggle against this system. When thus a wave of unrest goes through the land, when "it is in the air," when many join the cause, then in a great final effort this system can be shaken off. After all, an end in terror is preferable to terror without end.

We are not in a position to draw up a final judgment about the meaning of our history. But if this catastrophe can be used to further the public welfare, it will be only by virtue of the fact that we are cleansed by suffering; that we yearn for the light in the midst of deepest night, summon our strength, and finally help in shaking off the yoke which weighs on our world.

We do not want to discuss here the question of the Jews, nor do we want in this leaflet to compose a defense or apology. No, only by way of example do we want to cite the fact that since the conquest of Poland *three hundred thousand* Jews have been murdered in this country in the most bestial way. Here we see the most frightful crime against human dignity, a crime that is unparalleled in the whole of history. For Jews, too, are human beings—no matter what position we take with respect to the Jewish question—and a crime of this dimension has been perpetrated against human beings. Someone may say that the Jews deserved their fate. This assertion would be a monstrous impertinence; but let us assume that someone said this—what position has he then taken toward the fact that the entire Polish aristocratic youth is being annihilated? (May God grant that this program has not fully achieved its aim as yet!) All male offspring of the houses of the nobility between the ages of fifteen and twenty were transported to concentration camps in Germany and sentenced to forced labor, and all girls of this age group were sent to Norway, into the bordellos of the SS! Why tell you these things, since you are fully aware of them—or if not of these, then of other equally grave crimes committed by this frightful sub-humanity? Because here we touch on a problem which involves us deeply and forces us all to take thought. Why do the German people behave so apathetically in the face of all these abominable crimes, crimes so unworthy of the human race? Hardly anyone thinks about that. It is accepted as fact and put out of mind. The German people slumber on in their dull, stupid sleep and encourage these fascist criminals; they give them the opportunity to carry on their depredations; and of course they do so. Is this a sign that the Germans are brutalized in their simplest human feelings, that no chord within them cries out at the sight of such deeds, that they have sunk into a fatal consciencelessness from which they will never, never awake? It seems to be so, and will certainly be so, if the German does not at last start up out of his stupor, if he does not protest wherever and whenever he can against this clique of criminals, if he shows no sympathy for these hundreds of thousands of victims. He must evidence not only sympathy; no, much more: a sense of *complicity* in guilt. For through his apathetic behavior he gives these evil men the opportunity to act as they do; he tolerates this "government" which has taken upon itself such an infinitely great burden of guilt; indeed, he himself is to blame for the fact that it came about at all! Each man wants to be exonerated of a guilt of this kind, each one continues on his way with the most placid, the calmest conscience. But he cannot be exonerated; he is *guilty, guilty, guilty!* It is not too late, however, to do away with this most reprehensible of all miscarriages of government, so as to avoid being burdened with even greater guilt. Now, when in recent years our eyes have been opened, when we know exactly who our adversary is, it is high time to root out this brown horde. Up until the outbreak of the war the larger part of the German people was blinded; the Nazis did not show themselves in their true aspect. But now, now that we have recognized them for what they are, it must be the sole and first duty, the holiest duty of every German to destroy these beasts.

If the people are barely aware that the government exists, they are happy. When the government is felt to be oppressive, they are broken.

Good fortune, alas! builds itself upon misery. Good fortune, alas! is the mask of misery. What will come of this? We cannot foresee the end. Order is upset and turns to disorder, good becomes evil. The people are confused. Is it not so, day in, day out, from the beginning?

The wise man is therefore angular, though he does not injure others; he has sharp corners, though he does not harm; he is upright but not gruff. He is clear-minded, but he does not try to be brilliant.

Lao-tzu

Whoever undertakes to rule the kingdom and to shape it according to his whim—I foresee that he will fail to reach his goal. That is all.

The kingdom is a living being. It cannot be constructed, in truth! He who tries to manipulate it will spoil it, he who tries to put it under his power will lose it.

Therefore: Some creatures go out in front, others follow, some have warm breath, others cold, some are strong, some weak, some attain abundance, others succumb.

The wise man will accordingly forswear excess, he will avoid arrogance and not overreach.

Lao-tzu

Please make as many copies as possible of this leaflet and distribute them.

Salus publica suprema lex

All ideal forms of government are utopias. A state cannot be constructed on a purely theoretical basis; rather, it must grow and ripen in the way an individual human being matures. But we must not forget that at the starting point of every civilization the state was already there in rudimentary form. The family is as old as man himself, and out of this initial bond man, endowed with reason, created for himself a state founded on justice, whose highest law was the common good. The state should exist as a parallel to the divine order, and the highest of all utopias, the *civitas dei*, is the model which in the end it should approximate. Here we will not pass judgment on the many possible forms of the state—democracy, constitutional monarchy, monarchy, and so on. But one matter needs to be brought out clearly and unambiguously. Every individual human being has a claim to a useful and just state, a state which secures the freedom of the individual as well as the good of the whole. For, according to God's will, man is intended to pursue his natural goal, his earthly happiness, in self-reliance and self-chosen activity, freely and independently within the community of life and work of the nation.

But our present "state" is the dictatorship of evil. "Oh, we've known that for a long time," I hear you object, "and it isn't necessary to bring that to our attention again." But, I ask you, if you know that, why do you not bestir yourselves, why do you allow these men who are in power to rob you step by step, openly and in secret, of one domain of your rights after another, until one day nothing, nothing at all will be left but a mechanized state system presided over by criminals and drunks? Is your spirit already so crushed by abuse that you forget it is your right—or rather, your *moral duty*—to eliminate this system? But if a man no longer can summon the strength to demand his right, then it is absolutely certain that he will perish. We would deserve to be dispersed through the earth like dust before the wind if we do not muster our powers at this late hour and finally find the courage which up to now we have lacked. Do not hide your cowardice behind a cloak of expediency, for with every new day that you hesitate, failing to oppose this offspring of Hell, your guilt, as in a parabolic curve, grows higher and higher.

Many, perhaps most, of the readers of these leaflets do not see clearly how they can practice an effective opposition. They do not see any avenues open to them. We want to try to show them that everyone is in a position to contribute to the overthrow of this system. It is not possible through solitary withdrawal, in the manner of embittered hermits, to prepare the ground for the overturn of this "government" or bring about the revolution at the earliest possible moment. No, it can be done only by the cooperation of many convinced, energetic people—people who are agreed as to the means they must use to attain their goal. We have no great number of choices as to these means. The only one available is *passive resistance*. The meaning and the goal of passive resistance is to topple National Socialism, and in this struggle we must not recoil from any course, any action, whatever its nature. At *all* points we must oppose National Socialism, wherever it is open to attack. We must soon bring this monster of a state to an end. A victory of fascist Germany in this war would have immeasurable, frightful consequences. The military victory over Bolshevism dare not become the primary concern of the Germans. The defeat of the Nazis must *unconditionally* be the first order of business. The greater necessity of this latter requirement will be discussed in one of our forthcoming leaflets.

82

And now every convinced opponent of National Socialism must ask himself how he can fight against the present "state" in the most effective way, how he can strike it the most telling blows. Through passive resistance, without a doubt. We cannot provide each man with the blueprint for his acts, we can only suggest them in general terms, and he alone will find the way of achieving this end:

Sabotage in armament plants and war industries, sabotage at all gatherings, rallies, public ceremonies, and organizations of the National Socialist Party. Obstruction of the smooth functioning of the war machine (a machine for war that goes on solely to shore up and perpetuate the National Socialist Party and its dictatorship). *Sabotage* in all the areas of science and scholarship which further the continuation of the war—whether in universities, technical schools, laboratories, research institutes, or technical bureaus. *Sabotage* in all cultural institutions which could potentially enhance the "prestige" of the fascists among the people. *Sabotage* in all branches of the arts which have even the slightest dependence on National Socialism or render it service. *Sabotage* in all publications, all newspapers, that are in the pay of the "government" and that defend its ideology and aid in disseminating the brown lie. Do not give a penny to public drives (even when they are conducted under the pretense of charity). For this is only a disguise. In reality the proceeds aid neither the Red Cross nor the needy. The government does not need this money; it is not financially interested in these money drives. After all, the presses run continuously to manufacture any desired amount of paper currency. But the populace must be kept constantly under tension, the pressure of the bit must not be allowed to slacken! Do not contribute to the collections of metal, textiles, and the like. Try to convince all your acquaintances, including those in the lower social classes, of the senselessness of continuing, of the hopelessness of this war;

of our spiritual and economic enslavement at the hands of the National Socialists; of the destruction of all moral and religious values; and urge them to *passive resistance*!

Aristotle, *Politics*: " . . . and further, it is part [of the nature of tyranny] to strive to see to it that nothing is kept hidden of that which any subject says or does, but that everywhere he will be spied upon, . . . and further, to set man against man and friend against friend, and the common people against the privileged and the wealthy. Also it is part of these tyrannical measures, to keep the subjects poor, in order to pay the guards and soldiers, and so that they will be occupied with earning their livelihood and will have neither leisure nor opportunity to engage in conspiratorial acts. . . . Further, [to levy] such taxes on income as were imposed in Syracuse, for under Dionysius the citizens gladly paid out their whole fortunes in taxes within five years. Also, the tyrant is inclined constantly to foment wars."

Please duplicate and distribute!

There is an ancient maxim that we repeat to our children: "He who won't listen will have to feel." But a wise child will not burn his fingers the second time on a hot stove. In the past weeks Hitler has chalked up successes in Africa and in Russia. In consequence, optimism on the one hand and distress and pessimism on the other have grown within the German people with a rapidity quite inconsistent with traditional German apathy. On all sides one hears among Hitler's opponents—the better segments of the population—exclamations of despair, words of disappointment and discouragement, often ending with the question: "Will Hitler now, after all . . . ?"

Meanwhile the German offensive against Egypt has ground to a halt. Rommel has to bide his time in a dangerously exposed position. But the push into the East proceeds. This apparent success has been purchased at the most horrible expense of human life, and so it can no longer be counted an advantage. Therefore we must warn against *all* optimism.

Neither Hitler nor Goebbels can have counted the dead. In Russia thousands are lost daily. It is the time of the harvest, and the reaper cuts into the ripe grain with wide strokes. Mourning takes up her abode in the country cottages, and there is no one to dry the tears of the mothers. Yet Hitler feeds with lies those people whose most precious belongings he has stolen and whom he has driven to a meaningless death.

Every word that comes from Hitler's mouth is a lie. When he says peace, he means war, and when he blasphemously uses the name of the Almighty, he means the power of evil, the fallen angel, Satan. His mouth is the foul-smelling maw of Hell, and his might is at bottom accursed. True, we must conduct the struggle against the National

Socialist terrorist state with rational means; but whoever today still doubts the reality, the existence of demonic powers, has failed by a wide margin to understand the metaphysical background of this war. Behind the concrete, the visible events, behind all objective, logical considerations, we find the irrational element: the struggle against the demon, against the servants of the Antichrist. Everywhere and at all times demons have been lurking in the dark, waiting for the moment when man is weak; when of his own volition he leaves his place in the order of Creation as founded for him by God in freedom; when he yields to the force of evil, separates himself from the powers of a higher order; and, after voluntarily taking the first step, he is driven on to the next and the next at a furiously accelerating rate. Everywhere and at all times of greatest trial men have appeared, prophets and saints who cherished their freedom, who preached the One God and who with His help brought the people to a reversal of their downward course. Man is free, to be sure, but without the true God he is defenseless against the principle of evil. He is a like rudderless ship, at the mercy of the storm, an infant without his mother, a cloud dissolving into thin air.

I ask you, you as a Christian wrestling for the preservation of your greatest treasure, whether you hesitate, whether you incline toward intrigue, calculation, or procrastination in the hope that someone else will raise his arm in your defense? Has God not given you the strength, the will to fight? We *must* attack evil where it is strongest, and it is strongest in the power of Hitler.

So I returned, and considered all the oppressions that are done under the sun: and behold the tears of such as were oppressed, and they had no comforter; and on the side of their oppressors there was power; but they had no comforter.

Wherefore I praised the dead which are already
dead more than the living which are yet alive.

ECCLESIASTES 4.

True anarchy is the generative element of religion.
Out of the annihilation of every positive element she
lifts her gloriously radiant countenance as the founder
of a new world. . . . If Europe were about to awaken
again, if a state of states, a teaching of political science
were at hand! Should hierarchy then . . . be the principle of the union of states? Blood will stream over
Europe until the nations become aware of the frightful
madness which drives them in circles. And then, struck
by celestial music and made gentle, they approach
their former altars all together, hear about the works
of peace, and hold a great celebration of peace with
fervent tears before the smoking altars. Only religion
can reawaken Europe, establish the rights of the peoples, and install Christianity in new splendor visibly
on earth in its office as guarantor of peace.

NOVALIS

We wish expressly to point out that the White Rose is
not in the pay of any foreign power. Though we know that
National Socialist power must be broken by military means,
we are trying to achieve a renewal from within of the
severely wounded German spirit. This rebirth must be
preceded, however, by the clear recognition of all the guilt
with which the German people have burdened themselves,
and by an uncompromising battle against Hitler and his
all too many minions, party members, Quislings, and the
like. With total brutality the chasm that separates the
better portion of the nation from everything that is identified
with National Socialism must be opened wide. For Hitler
and his followers there is no punishment on this earth
commensurate with their crimes. But out of love for coming

generations we must make an example after the conclusion of the war, so that no one will ever again have the slightest urge to try a similar action. And do not forget the petty scoundrels in this regime; note their names, so that none will go free! They should not find it possible, having had their part in these abominable crimes, at the last minute to rally to another flag and then act as if nothing had happened!

To set you at rest, we add that the addresses of the readers of the White Rose are not recorded in writing. They were picked at random from directories.

We will not be silent. We are your bad conscience. The White Rose will not leave you in peace!

A Call to All Germans!

The war is approaching its destined end. As in the year 1918, the German government is trying to focus attention exclusively on the growing threat of submarine warfare, while in the East the armies are constantly in retreat and invasion is imminent in the West. Mobilization in the United States has not yet reached its climax, but already it exceeds anything that the world has ever seen. It has become a mathematical certainty that Hitler is leading the German people into the abyss. *Hitler cannot win the war; he can only prolong it.* The guilt of Hitler and his minions goes beyond all measure. Retribution comes closer and closer.

But what are the German people doing? They will not see and will not listen. Blindly they follow their seducers into ruin. *Victory at any price!* is inscribed on their banner. "I will fight to the last man," says Hitler—but in the meantime the war has already been lost.

Germans! Do you and your children want to suffer the same fate that befell the Jews? Do you want to be judged by the same standards as your traducers? Are we to be forever the nation which is hated and rejected by all mankind? No. Dissociate yourselves from National Socialist gangsterism. Prove by your deeds that you think otherwise. A new war of liberation is about to begin. The better part of the nation will fight on our side. Cast off the cloak of indifference you have wrapped around you. Make the decision *before it is too late!* Do not believe the National Socialist propaganda which has driven the fear of Bolshevism into your bones. Do not believe that Germany's welfare is linked to the victory of National Socialism for good or ill. A criminal regime cannot achieve a German victory. Separate yourselves *in time* from everything connected with National Socialism. In the aftermath a terrible but just judgment will be meted out to those who stayed in hiding, who were cowardly and hesitant.

What can we learn from the outcome of this war—this war that never was a national war?

The imperialist ideology of force, from whatever side it comes, must be shattered for all time. A one-sided Prussian militarism must never again be allowed to assume power. Only in large-scale cooperation among the nations of Europe can the ground be prepared for reconstruction. Centralized hegemony, such as the Prussian state has tried to exercise in Germany and in Europe, must be cut down at its inception. The Germany of the future must be a federal state. At this juncture only a sound federal system can imbue a weakened Europe with a new life. The workers must be liberated from their condition of down-trodden slavery under National Socialism. The illusory structure of autonomous national industry must disappear. Every nation and each man have a right to the goods of the whole world!

Freedom of speech, freedom of religion, the protection of individual citizens from the arbitrary will of criminal regimes of violence—these will be the bases of the New Europe.

Support the resistance. Distribute the leaflets!

Fellow Fighters in the Resistance!

Shaken and broken, our people behold the loss of the men of Stalingrad. Three hundred and thirty thousand German men have been senselessly and irresponsibly driven to death and destruction by the inspired strategy of our World War I Private First Class. Führer, we thank you!

The German people are in ferment. Will we continue to entrust the fate of our armies to a dilettante? Do we want to sacrifice the rest of German youth to the base ambitions of a Party clique? No, never! The day of reckoning has come—the reckoning of German youth with the most abominable tyrant our people have ever been forced to endure. In the name of German youth we demand restitution by Adolf Hitler's state of our personal freedom, the most precious treasure that we have, out of which he has swindled us in the most miserable way.

We grew up in a state in which all free expression of opinion is unscrupulously suppressed. The Hitler Youth, the SA, the SS have tried to drug us, to revolutionize us, to regiment us in the most promising young years of our lives. "Philosophical training" is the name given to the despicable method by which our budding intellectual development is muffled in a fog of empty phrases. A system of selection of leaders at once unimaginably devilish and narrow-minded trains up its future party bigwigs in the "Castles of the Knightly Order" to become Godless, impudent, and conscienceless exploiters and executioners—blind, stupid hangers-on of the Führer. We "Intellectual Workers" are the ones who should put obstacles in the path of this caste of overlords. Soldiers at the front are regimented like schoolboys by student leaders and trainees for the post of Gauleiter, and the lewd jokes of the Gauleiters insult the honor of the women students. German women students at the university in Munich have given a dignified reply to the besmirching of their honor, and German students have defended the women in the universities and have stood firm. . . . That is a beginning of the struggle for our free self-determination—without which intellectual and spiritual values cannot be created. We thank the brave comrades, both men and women, who have set us a brilliant example.

For us there is but one slogan: fight against the party! Get out of the party organizations, which are used to keep our mouths sealed and hold us in political bondage! Get out of the lecture rooms of the SS corporals and sergeants and the party bootlickers! We want genuine learning and real freedom of opinion. No threat can terrorize us, not even the shutting down of the institutions of higher learning. This is the struggle of each and every one of us for our future, our freedom, and our honor under a regime conscious of its moral responsiblity.

Freedom and honor! For ten long years Hitler and his coadjutors have manhandled, squeezed, twisted, and debased these two splendid German words to the point of nausea, as only dilettantes can, casting the highest values of a nation before swine. They have sufficiently demonstrated in the ten years of destruction of all material and intellectual freedom, of all moral substance among the German people, what they understand by freedom and honor. The frightful bloodbath has opened the eyes of even the stupidest German—it is a slaughter which they arranged in the name of "freedom and honor of the German nation" throughout Europe, and which they daily start anew. The name of Germany is dishonored for all time if German youth does not finally rise, take revenge, and atone, smash its tormentors, and set up a new Europe of the spirit. Students! The German people look to us. As in 1813 the people expected us to shake off the Napoleonic yoke, so in 1943 they look to us to break the National Socialist terror through the power of the spirit. Beresina and Stalingrad are burning in the East. The dead of Stalingrad implore us to take action.

"Up, up, my people, let smoke and flame be our sign!"

Our people stand ready to rebel against the National Socialist enslavement of Europe in a fervent new breakthrough of freedom and honor.

Concluding Remarks (1969)

This book was written in 1947 for use in the schools, for adolescents from the age of thirteen to eighteen. It was addressed to the young people who had grown up in the Hitler Youth and had experienced the great disappointment of their lives as a result of the Second World War—children who at that time were asking their parents, "How was it possible for you to be taken in by the Nazis?" It was written also for those of their elders who were ready to face up to their past. Because of the circumstances of its publication, this book may have occasioned some misunderstanding; it requires a word in conclusion.

Written as it was for young people, it may have failed to do justice to the political dimension; it is easy to assume that the young are not interested in history and lack political insight. Similarly, one may be inclined today to see in the Munich resistance of 1943 little more than an action arising out of moral outrage—a spontaneous outburst, whose political aspects the resisters themselves had not taken fully into account.

To correct such possible misconceptions, I should like in these remarks to treat two questions. What were the intentions of these members of the resistance? What is the relation between their acts and the restlessness and rebellion of students generally?

All the members of the Munich resistance were undoubtedly aware that only the use of force could topple the governing regime with its apparatus of total power. Since force was not available, they chose another path of opposition—the way of disseminating information and enlightenment, and of fostering passive resistance. Whether they looked forward to or hoped concretely for a turn to active resistance in the latter stages of the struggle is of no moment. In any case, they wrote in the second leaflet of the White Rose: "When thus a wave of unrest goes through the land, when 'it is in the air,' when many join the cause, then in a great final effort this system can be shaken off. After all, an end in terror is preferable to terror without end." Furthermore, some of the resisters were engaged in accumulating a supply of weapons.

What the circle of the White Rose strove for was increasing public consciousness of the real nature and actual situation of National Socialism. They wanted to encourage passive resistance among wide circles of the populace. In the circumstances, a tight, closely knit organization would not have succeeded. The panicked fear of the people in the face of the constant threat of Gestapo intervention and the ubiquity and thoroughness of the surveillance system were the strongest obstacles. On the other hand, it still seemed possible, by means of anonymous dissemination of information, to create the impression that the Führer no longer enjoyed solid support and that there was general ferment— "Es brodelte an allen Ecken und Enden," as a respected member of the intellectual group in Munich remarked at that time. The demand for passive resistance was intended to give a palpable if invisible sense of solidarity to the isolated individuals of the opposition, to strengthen them and increase their numbers. It was intended to win over the hesitant, to move the uncommitted to a decision, to cast doubt in the minds of Nazi followers, to induce questioning in the minds of Nazi enthusiasts. Passive resistance, for which the leaflets called in such insistent and imploring terms, boasted no great arsenal of possibilities, but the few

95

that were available were intended to be mobilized. These included the resistance implicit in personal training in civil courage (for example, failing to give the Fascist salute when a column of Brown Shirts with their flag marched by); even going so far as withdrawing from the Party or from the Hitler Youth or passing on information by whispering campaigns. Such acts demanded extraordinary courage and could easily lead to one's being branded an "enemy of the people." Since Hitler's moods were said to be extraordinarily dependent on the sympathy of the masses, a reversal of feeling among the populace would have been a weapon of considerable force against him, one which would threaten his own self-confidence. For these reasons the leaflets of the White Rose were held by the highest levels of the party to constitute one of the greatest political "crimes" against the Third Reich.

For a nonpolitical German (and as a rule the Germans were nonpolitical) passive resistance meant more or less the following: Keeping apart from everything that was associated with National Socialism; withholding of support, direct or indirect, from the National Socialist Party; help for the oppressed; help for the Jews, wherever that was still possible; expressing solidarity with foreign forced laborers and prisoners of war; practicing acts of noncooperation and training oneself for a covert boycott; being conscious of oneself as a link in a great chain of European resistance reaching from France through Holland, Belgium, and Scandinavia to Eastern Europe. This solidarity with the other European resistance groups was apparently of great moment to my brother; he saw the war as the final stage of a nationalism which in itself tends almost inevitably to pass over into fascism. For this reason, according to the report of a survivor, he and his friends avoided the term "German" in the title of the next-to-last leaflet, heading it simply "Leaflet of the Resistance."

What the resisters understood by passive resistance is stated in the third leaflet:

> We have no great number of choices as to these means. The only one available is *passive resistance*.
>
> The meaning and goal of passive resistance is to topple National Socialism, and in this struggle we must not recoil from any course, any action, whatever its nature. At *all* points we must oppose National Socialism, wherever it is open to attack. We must soon bring this monster of a state to an end. A victory of fascist Germany in this war would have immeasurable, frightful consequences. . . .
>
> And now every convinced opponent of National Socialism must ask himself how he can fight against the present "state" in the most effective way, how he can strike the most telling blows. Through passive resistance, without a doubt. We cannot provide each man with the blueprint for his acts, we can only suggest them in general terms, and he will find the way of achieving this end:
>
> *Sabotage* in armament plants and war industries. Sabotage at all gatherings, rallies, public ceremonies, and organizations of the National Socialist Party. Obstruction of the smooth functioning of the war machine (a machine for war that goes on *solely* to shore up and perpetuate the National Socialist Party and its dictatorship). *Sabotage* in all the areas of science and scholarship which further the continuation of the war—whether in universities, technical schools, laboratories, research institutes, or technical bureaus. *Sabotage* in all cultural institutions which could potentially enhance the "prestige" of the fascists among the people. *Sabotage* in all branches of the arts . . . . Do not give a penny to public drives . . . . Do not contribute to the collections

of metal, textiles, and the like. Try to convince all your acquaintances (including those in the lower social classes) of the senselessness of continuing, of the hopelessness of this war; of our intellectual and economic enslavement at the hands of the National Socialists; of the destruction of all moral and religious values; and urge them to *passive resistance*!

We should not read into their persuasive call to passive resistance any inclination to indulge in activism for its own sake; for even though it were entered into wholeheartedly, it would be ineffective. Nor does it mean that they shrank from soiling their hands with unpleasant tasks. These students saw passive resistance as the art of the possible, an art which everyone can practice and which at the same time is the most exacting demand that society makes of the citizen. They meant to move by small stages (wherever this would promote a forward development) rather than to issue great, or even brilliant, rhetorical proclamations; to concentrate upon what was attainable, always keeping the ultimate goal in view.

Theirs was the voice of the independent man as the traditions of humanism, the Enlightenment, and early socialism had envisioned him. He was the basis for the envisaged foundation of the republican form of the state—the individual as the autonomous, nonmanipulable core of a free society. It was the voice of the man who was not ready to delegate his right of opinion to organizations which did not wholly represent his own views. This uprising of the single man is a specific characteristic of these students, as is the fact that they sought ways of combating a dictatorship even when the prospects of success were slight.

One characteristic of the German resistance was that it gave the appearance of having to oppose its own state, its people, and that people's interests. For many, this entailed a difficult conflict, through which they struggled with effort. But not so for my brother and sister; for them no dilemma existed. Behind the resistance of the other European nations against the fascist-German occupation power stood the solidarity of each of their respective peoples. In Germany this was not the case. However, the absence of this solidarity with one's own people crystallized all the more clearly something of first importance—a core of resistance against fascism itself. Above all, there were the human and humanitarian values that had to be preserved. It was a matter of defending a free society, an order which in the centuries preceding our era had had to be won with great effort and sacrifice. It was a matter of putting up a defense against the imminent threat of a new barbarism, against the legalization of genocide, and against the piratical-elitist doctrine of the race and of the state.

The defense of common humanity everywhere had to be raised above the interest of the nation. The common interest of all nations and races was greater and immeasurably more important than the differences among people, and it had therefore to be rescued. In a war against the individual, against people different from ourselves, and against dissident minorities, the resisters had to show their solidarity with these isolated individuals. The oppression by the national state—speaking, as it did, in its egocentric way in the name of the whole nation—thus caused a new sense of community to grow on a higher level.

The resisters' political position was initially to support generally the idea of parliamentary democracy, particularly in its Anglo-Saxon form. But this aspect did not occupy the foreground. The decisive matter for them was their movement away from an affirmation of the National-Socialist regime to a position of criticism. Out of their gradually developed sense of uncertainty grew a massive negation, which finally found its outlet, not in a weighing of theoretical alternatives, but in the will to bring about change.

Of course politics became more and more a theoretical passion. Hans Scholl toyed with the idea of changing from medicine to history and political journalism. Nevertheless the image, the idea, of what was to come *afterward* was more a presentiment than a firm concept. Perhaps it might happen that the defeat of Nazism from within the nation would in time show the way to a program for the future.

Nationalism, particularly in its bourgeois form, had been rejected by these students almost disrespectfully. In their awareness of this fact they undoubtedly tried, especially in their first leaflet, to hide their true opinion, so as not to spoil its effect. They conspicuously quoted and referred to some of the great Germans of the past because they hoped to stir a response particularly among German intellectuals. Out of their familiarity with intellectuals and the feeling that the educated middle classes had failed in their responsibility, they tried to arouse a bad conscience and to kindle an inner as well as an overt protest.

Further, they did not agree at all that the opposition to Hitler should be equated with anti-Communism. On this point they held excited debates. Among the opponents of Nazism in Germany there were many who supported the liberal ideas of the Western Powers and at the same time preached a crusade against Bolshevism. Many even hoped to make political capital out of this point, expecting England and the United States to show an interest in having the Germans as partners in an alliance against the East. (This, of course, is the situation that came about shortly after the war.)

The political instincts of my brother and sister were (and so not wholly unlike the student opposition of today) socially rather than ideologically oriented. In the foreground stood the failure of the German intellectuals. In a diary entry of my brother's dated in the autumn of 1942—

100

while he was serving on the Russian front as medical aide—he wrote: "Man is born to think, says Pascal; to think, my honored academic. I take this statement to be your reproach. You are surprised, representative of the intellect! But it is the very negation of the intellect that you serve in this desperate hour. You do not see the despair. You are rich, you do not see the poor. Your soul is dried up because you did not want to heed its call. You apply your intellect to the refinement of a machine gun, but even in your young years you brushed aside the simplest, the primary questions: Why? and Whither?"

In my brother's opinion, the intellectuals, because of their knowledge, had the greater responsibility, but at the same time they were more confused and more at a loss than, say, the workers or the clergy. Now it was necessary, from within the university itself, not only to carry on discussion, but through action to move this social elite onto new ground—that is, to change the role of the German intellectuals to one of political *engagement*.

Such rigor of thought was doubtless closely related to their discovery of Christianity, which in the case of my brother and sister paralleled the development of their independent political stand. The church hierarchy in those years had compromised itself by its initial alliance with National Socialism, and it was silent. But countless Christians had gone underground and some had joined the resistance. Thus a pathway was opened that led to Christianity—a path not blocked by any irrelevant acts of the Church. Through such friends and writers as Carl Muth and Theodor Haecker the young people participated in the existentialist dialogue centering on Kierkegaard, Augustine, and Pascal. On the other hand, the newly rediscovered rationalism of the medieval scholastics provided the base for an analogy between the modern world and religion. Unlike the situation a few years later, in the conservative era of Adenauer, these people were conscious of the fact that the West and Western civilization were passing into obsolescence. A dialogue between Maritain and Jean Cocteau on theology and surrealism was most compelling, particularly as these young people were at that moment discovering James Joyce, Georges Braque, and Franz Marc—all of whom they saw as the forbidden harbingers of a freer world. It was one of the unusual circumstances of the time that a line of relationship could exist between the expressionist painters, modern theology, and political activism. Another decisive factor was that they did not have to live at second hand. They visited artists in their studios, for they were not otherwise accessible; their paintings were proscribed. They met philosophers and engaged them in discussion; their books were not offered for sale. They were present at the moment when ideas were born, not after they had become articles of consumption. Thus they developed the freedom and progressive cast of thought which ultimately forced them to act.

It would be wrong to see the action of the students in Munich in the period 1942–1943 as a noble deed in the abstract. It was concrete, and its goal and starting point were concrete. To this extent it would also be wrong to understand their action as symbolic, even though many persons would like to draw support from examples of action such as theirs. It would be equally wrong to work out elaborate connections between what they did then and what students are doing today. The goals and circumstances are fundamentally different.

It does not diminish the significance of these students of 1942–1943 if we see them as a historically limited phenomenon. To what is happening today there are at best only analogies. Though again and again people have tried to establish parallels, it is my view that one should let what happened then stand as it was. Practical applications do not exist; we should look upon it as a singular instance.

It was an instance in which five or six students took it upon themselves to act while the dictatorship was totally in control; in which they accepted the lonely burden of not even being able to discuss these matters with their families; in which they took action even though the omnipotent state allowed them no room for maneuver; in which they acted in spite of the fact that they could do no more than tear small rifts in the structure of that state—much less blast out the cornerstones.

It is rare that a man is prepared to pay with his life for such a minimal achievement as causing cracks in the edifice of the existing order.

Documents

DOCUMENT 1. Indictment of Hans and Sophie Scholl and Christoph Probst as drawn up by the Reich Attorney General to the People's Court, February 21, 1943.

February 21, 1943
Berlin

Reich Attorney General
to the People's Court

H = Regular Volume
S = Supplementary Volume

Indictment

S v. 2   1. *Hans* Fritz *Scholl* of Munich, born September 22, 1918, in Ingersheim, single, no previous convictions, taken into investigative custody on February 18, 1943;

S v. 1   2. *Sophia* Magdalena *Scholl* of Munich, born on May 9, 1921, in Forchtenberg, single, no previous convictions, taken into investigative custody on February 18, 1943; and

  3. *Christoph* Hermann *Probst* of Aldrans bei Innsbruck, born on November 6, 1919, in Murnau, married, no previous convictions, taken into investigative custody February 20, 1943;

all at present in the jail of the headquarters, State Police (Gestapo), Munich,

all at present not represented by counsel;

are accused:

in 1942 and 1943 in Munich, Augsburg, Salzburg, Vienna, Stuttgart, and Linz, committing together the same acts:

I. with attempted high treason, namely by force to change the constitution of the Reich, and acting with intent:

1. to organize a conspiracy for the preparation of high treason,

2. to render the armed forces unfit for the performance of their duty of protecting the German Reich against internal and external attack,

3. to influence the masses through the preparation and distribution of writings; and

II. with having attempted, in the internal area of the Reich, during time of war, to give aid to the enemy against the Reich, injuring the war potential of the Reich; and

III. with having attempted to cripple and weaken the will of the German people to take measures toward their defense and self-determination,

Crimes according to Par. 80, Sec. 2; Par 83, Secs. 2 and 3, No. 1, 2, 3; Pars. 91b, 47, 73 of the Reich Criminal Code (St GB), and Par. 5 of the Special War Criminal Decree.

In the summer of 1942 and in January and February of 1943 the accused Hans *Scholl* prepared and distributed leaflets containing the demand for a settlement of accounts with National Socialism, for disaffection from the National Socialist "gangsterism," and for passive resistance and sabotage. In addition, in Munich he adorned walls with the defamatory slogan "Down With Hitler" and with canceled swastikas. The accused Sophie *Scholl* participated in the preparation and distribution of the seditious materials. The accused *Probst* composed the first draft of a leaflet.

I

Summary of Results of Investigations

S I 4–R 1. To the year 1930 the father of the accused Hans and Sophie Scholl was mayor of Forchtenberg. Later he was Economic Adviser in Ulm on the Danube. The accused Scholls have two sisters and a brother, who is now serving in the armed forces. Against the accused Hans Scholl, as well as against his brother Werner and his sister Inge, charges had previously been brought on the part of the Reich Police Headquarters, Stuttgart, concerning conspiratorial acts, which led to the temporary arrest of the above-named. Hans Scholl attended the local secondary school and in 1937 he enlisted in the army. In 1939 he began his studies in medicine, which he continued during his period of active service in the army in April, 1941. He was last assigned to the Student Company in Munich with the rank of sergeant. He covered the cost of tuition out of his army pay and out of an allowance from his father. In 1933 Scholl joined the *Hitler Jungvolk* and was later transferred to the *Hitler Jugend*.

2. The accused Sophia Scholl worked first as kindergarten teacher and since the summer of 1942 has been studying science and philosophy at the University of Munich. Until 1941 she belonged to the *Bund deutscher Mädel*, serving finally as Group Leader.

3. The accused *Probst* attended the *Gymnasium* in Nuremberg and, after finishing his Labor Service, volunteered for the army. Later he became a medical student and most recently belonged to the Student Company in Innsbruck with the rank of sergeant in the medical service.

II

In the summer of 1942 the so-called Leaflets of the White Rose were distributed through the mails. These seditious pamphlets contain attacks on National Socialism and on its cultural-political policies in particular; further, they contain statements concerning the alleged atrocities of National Socialism, namely the alleged murder of the Jews and the alleged forced deportation of the Poles. In addition, the leaflets contain the demand "to obstruct the continued functioning of the atheistic war machine" by passive resistance, before it is too late and before the last of the German cities, like Cologne, become heaps of ruins and German youth has bled to death for the *"hubris* of a subhuman."* According to Leaflet No. II, a wave of unrest must go through the land. If "it is in the air," if many participate, then in a great final effort this system can be shaken off. An end with terror, the leaflet stated, is preferable to terror without end. In Leaflet No. III the idea is developed that it is the intent and goal of passive resistance to bring down National Socialism. In this struggle one should not hesitate to take any course, to do any deed. At all points National Socialism must be attacked, wherever it may be vulnerable. Not military victory should be the first concern of every German, but rather the defeat of National Socialism. Every committed opponent of National Socialism must therefore ask himself how he can most effectively struggle against the present "state" and deal it the most telling blows. To this end sabotage in armament plants and war industry, the obstruction of the smooth functioning of the war machine, and sabotage of all National Socialist functions, as well as in all areas of scientific and intellectual life, is demanded.

A total of four separate leaflets of this sort were distributed in Munich at that time.

In January and February of 1943 two separate seditious leaflets were distributed by means of random scattering and through the mails. One of these bears the heading "Leaflets of the Resistance Movement in Germany" and the other "Fellow Fighters in the Resistance!" or "German Students!" The first leaflet states that the war is approaching its sure and certain end. However, the German government is trying to direct all attention to the growing submarine threat, while in the East the armies are falling back ceaselessly in retreat, in the West the invasion is expected, and the armament of America is said to exceed anything that history has heretofore recorded. Hitler (it states) cannot win the war; he can only prolong it. The German people, who have blindly followed their seducers into ruin, should now dissociate themselves from National Socialist sub-humanity and through their deeds demonstrate that they do not agree. National Socialist propaganda, which has terrorized the people by fostering a fear of Bolshevism, should not be given credence, and people should not believe that Germany's future is tied to the victory of National Socialism for better or for worse.

The second leaflet, referring to the battle of the Sixth Army at Stalingrad, states that there is a ferment among the German people, and the question is raised whether the fate of our armies should be entrusted to a dilettante. The breaking of National Socialist terror, the leaflet expects, will be the work of students—to whom the German people are looking for guidance and who will achieve their goal through the power of the intellect.

III

1. The accused Hans *Scholl* occupied his thoughts for a long time with the political situation. He arrived at the conclusion that just as in 1918, so also after the seizure of power by the National Socialists in 1933, it was not» the majority of the German masses but the intellectuals in particular who had failed politically. This is the only explanation, in his opinion, why mass movements with simplistic slogans had succeeded in drowning out all thought that was more profound. Accordingly, he felt it his duty to remind the middle-class intellectuals of their political obligations, one of which was to take up the struggle against National Socialism. He therefore decided to prepare and distribute leaflets intended to carry his ideas to the broad masses of the people. He bought a duplicating machine, and with the help of a friend, Alexander *Schmorell*, with whom he had often discussed his political views, he acquired a typewriter. He then drafted the first leaflet of the "White Rose" and claims singlehandedly to have prepared about a hundred copies and to have mailed them to addresses chosen from the Munich telephone directory. In so doing, he selected people in academic circles particularly, but also restaurant owners who, he hoped, would spread the contents of the leaflets by word of mouth. Subsequently he prepared three additional leaflets of the "White Rose," which were likewise written by him. The contents of these leaflets are reproduced above, in Part II of this indictment. Again these were distributed through the mails.

He was prevented from issuing more writings by his assignment to active duty on the eastern front in July 1942. He claims that in part he himself paid for the materials used in preparing the leaflets; some portion of the costs were given to him, he claims, by his friend Schmorell.

The name "The White Rose," according to the statements of the accused Hans Scholl, was chosen arbitrarily and took its inception from his reading of a Spanish novel with this title. The accused claims that at first he did not plan an organization; only later, namely early in 1943, did he draw up the plan for an organization which was to propagate his ideas. He claims that he has not yet attempted to bring together a group of like-minded persons.

Early in 1943 the accused Hans Scholl—who in the meantime had been given leave from army service for the purpose of studying at the University of Munich, came to the conclusion—as he relates—that there was only one means of saving Europe, namely by shortening the war. To publicize this idea, he drafted two more leaflets, in editions totaling about 7,000, and with the titles mentioned above in Part II of this indictment. Of these he scattered about 5,000 copies in the inner city of Munich, and in addition he mailed numerous other copies. At the end of January he traveled to Salzburg, and from the railway post office he posted some 100 to 150 letters containing the leaflets he had prepared. In addition, about 1,500 of the seditious papers were distributed through the mails in Linz and Vienna by Schmorell, who at Scholl's behest traveled to these cities. Scholl contributed to the cost of train tickets. Finally Scholl had his sister Sophia take about 1,000 letters containing seditious leaflets to Augsburg and Stuttgart, where she put them in the mails. After the news of the reverses in the East, Hans Scholl again prepared leaflets in which he reproduced the text of his student leaflet under a new title. Of these he sent several hundred through the mails. He took the addresses from a directory of the University of Munich. On February 18, 1943, he and his sister also scattered more seditious papers. On this occasion he was observed by the witness *Schmied* and placed under arrest.

Early in 1943 the accused Hans Scholl requested his friend, the accused Probst (with whom he had for a long time exchanged ideas about the political situation), to write down his ideas on current developments. Probst then sent him a draft, which without doubt was to be duplicated and distributed, though there was no time for such action. This draft was found in Scholl's pocket at the time of his arrest.

At the end of January 1943 the accused Hans Scholl, at the suggestion of Schmorell, decided to make propaganda by painting defamatory slogans on walls. Schmorell pre-

Hans Scholl

pared a stencil for him with the text "Down With Hitler" and with a swastika which was canceled through, and he furnished paint and brush. In early February 1943 Hans Scholl, together with Schmorell, painted such slogans in black tar on several houses in Munich, on the columns in front of the University, on the buildings of the National Theater and the Ministry of Economics, the Schauspielhaus Theater, and elsewhere.

2. The accused Sophia *Scholl* as early as the summer of 1942 took part in political discussions, in which she and her brother, Hans Scholl, came to the conclusion that Germany had lost the war. Thus she shared with her brother the view that agitation against the war should be carried out through leaflets. She claims to be unable to remember whether the idea of the preparation of leaflets had its inception with her or with her brother. She claims that she had no part in the preparation and distribution of the leaflets with the title "The White Rose" and that she did not become aware of them until a friend showed her a copy. On the other hand, she admits to having taken part in preparing and distributing the leaflets in 1943. Together with her brother she drafted the text of the seditious "Leaflets of the Resistance in Germany." In addition, she had a part in the purchasing of paper, envelopes, and stencils, and together with her brother she actually prepared the duplicated copies of this leaflet. She also helped her brother address the envelopes for mailing. Furthermore, at the request of her brother she traveled by express train to Augsburg and Stuttgart and put the prepared letters into various mailboxes, and she took part in the distribution of the leaflets in Munich by depositing them in telephone booths and parked automobiles.

The accused Sophia Scholl was also implicated in the preparation and distribution of the student leaflets. She accompanied her brother to the university, was observed there in the act of scattering the leaflets, and was arrested when he was taken into custody.

The accused Sophia Scholl was not involved in the act of defacement of buildings, though when she learned about it, she offered to assist on future occasions. She even expressed the view to her brother that it might be a good form of concealment to have a woman taking part in this activity.

The accused Sophia Scholl knew that her brother spent considerable sums of money in the preparation of the seditious papers. In fact, she took charge of her brother's finances, since he was little concerned about money matters; she kept financial records and issued to him the sums he needed for these purposes.

3. The accused Probst, who was often in the company of brother and sister Scholl and who shared their ideas, wrote at the request of the accused Hans Scholl the draft, mentioned above, of his estimate of the current political scene. He claims, to be sure, that he did not know that Scholl intended to use the draft for a leaflet, but he did admit that he was aware that it might be used for illegal propaganda.

IV

The accused were on the whole willing to admit to their acts.

Testimony and Exhibits

I. The statements of the accused in the Supplementary Volumes I–III;

II. The Judge of the Police Praesidium of Munich: H 9 R;

III. The witnesses:

    1. Custodian Jakob Schmied, Munich, Türkenstrasse 33/I,

    2. and

    3. Officials of the Police yet to be named;

IV. Exhibits:

    1. The confiscated typewriters, duplicating machine, duplicating master, paint, and brushes;

    2. the leaflets and photographs in the appended volume of exhibits.

With the concurrence of the Chief of Staff of the Supreme Command of the Armed Services and the Reich Minister of Justice, the case is transferred to the People's Court for action and decision.

DOCUMENT 2. Transcript of the Sentence of Hans and Sophie Scholl and Christoph Probst, February 22, 1943.

Transcript
I H 47/43

In the Name
of the German People

In the action against

1. *Hans* Fritz *Scholl*, Munich, born at Ingersheim, September 22, 1918,
2. *Sophia* Magdalena *Scholl*, Munich, born at Forchtenberg, May 9, 1921, and
3. *Christoph* Hermann *Probst*, of Aldrans bei Innsbruck, born at Murnau, November 6, 1919,
   now in investigative custody regarding treasonous assistance to the enemy, preparing to commit high treason, and weakening of the nation's armed security,

the People's Court, first Senate, pursuant to the trial held on February 22, 1943, in which the officers were:

President of the People's Court Dr. Freisler, Presiding,
Director of the Regional (Bavarian) Judiciary Stier,
SS *Group Leader* Breithaupt,
SA *Group Leader* Bunge,
State Secretary and SA *Group Leader* Köglmaier, and, representing the Attorney General to the Supreme Court of the Reich, Reich Attorney Weyersberg,

find:

That the accused have in time of war by means of leaflets called for the sabotage of the war effort and armaments and for the overthrow of the National Socialist way of life of our people, have propagated defeatist ideas, and have most vulgarly defamed the Führer, thereby giving aid to the enemy of the Reich and weakening the armed security of the nation.

On this account they are to be punished by
Death.

Their honor and rights as citizens are forfeited for all time.

114

The accused Hans Scholl has been a student of medicine since the spring of 1939 and, thanks to the solicitude of the National Socialist government, has begun his eighth semester in those studies. He has served meanwhile on temporary duty in a field hospital in the campaign in France and again from July to November 1942 on the eastern front as a medical aide.

As a student he is bound by duty to give exemplary service to the common cause. In his capacity as soldier—on assignment to medical study—he has a special duty of loyalty to the Führer. This and the assistance which he was expressly granted by the Reich did not deter him in the first half of the summer of 1942 from writing, duplicating, and distributing leaflets of the "White Rose." These defeatist leaflets predict the defeat of Germany and call for passive resistance in the form of sabotage in war industries and for sabotage in general, to the end that the German people would be deprived of the National Socialist way of life and thus also of their government.

All this because he imagined that only in this way could the German people survive the end of the war!

Returning from Russia in November 1942, Scholl requested his friend, the accused Probst, to provide him with a manuscript which would open the eyes of the German people! In actuality Probst furnished Scholl with a draft of a leaflet as requested, at the end of January 1943.

In conversations with his sister, Sophia, the two decided to carry on leaflet propaganda in the form of a campaign against the war and in favor of collaboration with the plutocratic enemies of National Socialism. Brother and sister, who had quarters in the same rooming house, collaborated in the writing of a leaflet, "To All Germans." In it they predicted Germany's defeat in the war, they urged a war of liberation against "National Socialist gangsterism," and demanded the establishment of a liberal democracy. In addition, they drafted a leaflet, "German Students!" (in later versions, "Fellow Fighters!"), wherein they called for a struggle against the Party. They wrote that the day of reckoning was at hand, and they were bold enough to

115

compare their call to battle against the Führer and the National Socialist way of life with the War of Liberation against Napoleon (1813). In reference to their project, they used the military song, "Up, up, my people, let smoke and flame be our sign!"

The accused Scholls, in part with the help of the accused Schmorell, duplicated the leaflets and by common agreement distributed them as follows:

1. Schmorell traveled to Salzburg, Linz, and Vienna and put 200, 200, and 1,200 leaflets addressed to places in those cities in the mails; and in Vienna an additional 400 were directed to Frankfurt am Main.

2. Sophia Scholl posted 200 in Augsburg and on another occasion 600 in Stuttgart.

3. Hans Scholl, with the aid of Schmorell, scattered thousands of leaflets in the streets of Munich at night.

4. On February 18 the Scholls deposited 1500–1800 copies in bundles in the University of Munich, and Sophia Scholl let drop a large number from the third floor down the light well of the building.

Hans Scholl and Schmorell also, on the nights of August 8, 1942, and February 14, 1943, defaced walls in many places in Munich, and particularly the University, with the words "Down With Hitler," "Hitler the Mass Murderer," and "Freedom." After the first incident Sophia Scholl learned of this action, was in agreement with it, and requested—though without success—to be allowed to help in the future!

Expenses were covered by the accused themselves—in all, about 1,000 marks.

Probst likewise began his medical studies in the spring of 1939 and is now in his eighth semester, a soldier on student duty. He is married and has three children aged two and a half, one and one fourth years, and four weeks. He is a "nonpolitical man"—hence no man at all! Neither the solicitude of the National Socialist Reich for his professional training nor the fact that it was only the National Socialist demographic policy which made it possible for him to have a family prevented him from writing at the behest of Scholl—in cowardly defeatism—a "manuscript" which takes the heroic struggle in Stalingrad as the occasion for defaming the Führer as a military swindler and which then, progressing to a hortatory tone, calls for opposition to National Socialism and for action which would lead, as he pretends, to an honorable capitulation. He supports the promises in this leaflet by citing—Roosevelt! And his knowledge about these matters he derived from listening to British broadcasts!

All the accused have admitted the facts stated above. Probst offers as excuse his "psychotic depression" of the time he drafted the leaflet, a depression which he claims arises from Stalingrad and the childbed illness of his wife. But such explanations do not excuse a reaction *of this scope.*

Whoever has, like the three accused, committed the acts of high treason, weakening the home front and thereby in time of war the security of the nation, and by the same token has aided the enemy (Par. 5 of Special War Decree and Par. 91b of the Criminal Code), raises the dagger for a stab in the back of the Front! That applies also to Probst, though he claims that his manuscript was not intended for use as a leaflet—since the tone and style of the manuscript proves the opposite. Whoever acts in this way—and particularly at this time, when we must close our ranks—is attempting to cause the first rift in the unity of the battle front. And German students, whose traditional honor has always called for self-sacrifice for *Volk* and fatherland, were the ones who acted thus!

If a deed of this sort were to be punished otherwise than by death, we would be forging the first links of a chain whose end—in an earlier time—was 1918. Therefore, for the protection of the *Volk* and the Reich at war, the People's Court has found but one just punishment: death. The People's Court knows that it is at one with our soldiers in this decision.

Through their treason to our *Volk*, the accused have forever forfeited their citizenship.

As criminals who have been found guilty, the accused will pay the court costs.

Stier.

Dr. Freisler
(signed)

Certified True Copy
Landesarchiv Berlin
Berlin-Charlottenburg
December 22, 1960
(Seal)   (signature illegible)

D<small>OCUMENT</small> 3. Transcript of the Sentence of Alexander Schmorell, Kurt Huber, Wilhelm Graf, and Others Associated with the Resistance of the White Rose, Pursuant to the Trial Held on April 19, 1943.   Confidential

Transcript
6 J 24/43
1 II 101/43

In the Name
of the German People

In the action against

1. Alexander *Schmorell*, Munich, born on September 16, 1917, in Orenburg (Russia);
2. Kurt *Huber*, Munich, born October 24, 1893, in Chur (Switzerland);
3. Wilhelm *Graf*, Munich, born January 2, 1918, in Kuchenheim;
4. Hans *Hirzel*, Ulm, born on October 30, 1924, in Untersteinbach (Stuttgart);
5. Susanne *Hirzel*, Stuttgart, born on August 7, 1921, in Untersteinbach;
6. *Franz* Joseph *Müller*, Ulm, born on September 8, 1924, in Ulm;
7. Heinrich *Guter*, Ulm, born on January 11, 1925, in Ulm;
8. Eugen *Grimminger*, Stuttgart, born on July 29, 1892, in Crailsheim;
9. Dr. *Heinrich* Philipp *Bollinger*, Freiburg, born on April 23, 1916, in Saarbrücken;
10. *Helmut* Karl Theodore August *Bauer*, Freiburg, born on June 19, 1919, in Saarbrücken;
11. Dr. *Falk* Erich Walter *Harnack*, Chemnitz, born on March 2, 1913, in Stuttgart;
12. Gisela *Schertling*, Munich, born on February 9, 1922, in Pössneck (Thüringen);
13. Katharina *Schüddekopf*, Munich, born on February 8, 1916, in Magdeburg;
14. Traute *Lafrenz*, Munich, born on May 3, 1919, in Hamburg;

at present in investigative custody, regarding rendering aid to the enemy, inter alia, the People's Court, first Senate, pursuant to the trial held on April 19, 1943, in which the the officers were:

President of the People's Court Dr. Freisler, Presiding, Director of the Regional (Bavarian) Judiciary Stier, SS *Group Leader* and Lt. Gen. of the Waffen-SS Breithaupt,

SA *Group Leader* Bunge,

SA *Group Leader* and State Secretary Köglmaier, and, representing the Reich Attorney General, First State's Attorney Bischoff,

find:

That Alexander *Schmorell*, Kurt *Huber*, and Wilhelm *Graf* in time of war have promulgated leaflets calling for sabotage of the war effort and for the overthrow of the National Socialist way of life of our people; have propagated defeatist ideas, and have most vulgarly defamed the Führer, thereby giving aid to the enemy of the Reich and weakening the armed security of the nation.

On this account they are to be punished by *Death*.

Their honor and rights as citizens are forfeited for all time.

Eugen *Grimminger* gave money to a person guilty of high treason in aid of the enemy. To be sure, he was not aware that by so doing he was aiding the enemy of the Reich. However, he was aware that this person might use the money for the purpose of robbing our people of their National Socialist way of life.

Because he gave support to high treason, he is sentenced to jail for a ten-year term, together with loss of honorable estate for ten years.

Heinrich *Bollinger* and Helmut *Bauer* had knowledge of treasonable conspiracy but failed to report it. In addition, the two listened to foreign radio newscasts dealing with the war and with events inside Germany. For this they are sentenced to jail for a term of seven years and loss of citizen's honor for seven years.

Hans *Hirzel* and Franz *Müller*—both immature boys misled by enemies of the state—gave support to the spread of treasonous propaganda against National Socialism. For this action they are sentenced to five years' imprisonment.

120

Heinrich *Guter* had knowledge of propagandistic intentions of this sort but failed to report them. For this he is sentenced to eighteen months' imprisonment.

Gisela *Schertling*, Katharina *Schüddekopf*, and Traute *Lafrenz* committed the same crimes. As girls, they are sentenced to one year's imprisonment.

Susanne *Hirzel* assisted in the distribution of treasonous leaflets. To be sure, she was not aware of their treasonous nature, but she was guilty in that in her inexcusable credulousness and good faith she did not seek certainty concerning the matter. She is sentenced to six months' imprisonment.

In the case of all the accused who have been sentenced to jail or imprisonment, the People's Court will accept as part of the punishment the time already spent in police and investigative custody.

Falk *Harnack* likewise failed to report his knowledge of treasonous activity. But such unique and special circumstances surround his case that we find ourselves unable to punish his deed of omission. He is accordingly set free.

Grounds

These sentences must be considered in connection with those the People's Court was forced to render recently. At that time sentence was passed on three persons who, among others, formed the core of this treasonous assistance to our enemies. Two of these, Hans and Sophie Scholl, were the guiding spirits of a genuinely treasonous organization, set up in aid of the enemy and intended to weaken the armed security of the nation. They are members of a family which itself tended to be hostile to the interests of the people and which failed to give them the upbringing that would have formed them into decent citizens. At that time the People's Court arrived at the following determination with regard to their crime and guilt:

The accused Hans Scholl has been a student of medicine since the spring of 1939 and, thanks to the solicitude of the National Socialist government, has begun his eighth semester in those studies. He has served meanwhile on temporary duty in a field hospital in the campaign in France and again from July to

November 1942 on the eastern front as a medical aide. As a student he is bound by duty to give exemplary service to the common cause. In his capacity as soldier —on assignment to medical study—he has a special duty of loyalty to the Führer. This and the assistance which he was expressly granted by the Reich did not deter him in the first half of the summer of 1942 from writing, duplicating, and distributing leaflets of the "White Rose." These defeatist leaflets predict the defeat of Germany and call for passive resistance in the form of sabotage in war industries and for sabotage in general, to the end that the German people would be deprived of their National Socialist way of life and thus also of their government.

All this because he imagined that only in this way could the German people survive the end of the war!

Returning from Russia in November 1942, Scholl requested his friend, the accused Probst, to provide him with a manuscript which would open the eyes of the German people! In actuality Probst furnished Scholl with a draft of a leaflet as requested, at the end of January 1943.

In conversations with his sister, Sophia, the two decided to carry on leaflet propaganda in the form of a campaign against the war and in favor of collaboration with the plutocratic enemies of National Socialism. Brother and sister, who had quarters in the same rooming house, collaborated in the writing of a leaflet, "To All Germans." In it they predicted Germany's defeat in the war, they urged a war of liberation against "National Socialist gangsterism," and demanded the establishment of a liberal democracy. In addition, they drafted a leaflet, "German Students!" (in later versions, "Fellow Fighters!"), wherein they called for a struggle against the Party. They wrote that the day of reckoning was at hand, and they were bold enough to compare their call to battle against the Führer and the National Socialist way of life with the War of Liberation against Napoleon (1813). In reference to their project, they used the military song, "Up, up, my people, let smoke and flame be our sign!"

The accused Scholls, in part with the help of the accused Schmorell, duplicated the leaflets and by common agreement distributed them as follows:

1. Schmorell traveled to Salzburg, Linz, and Vienna and put 200, 200, and 1,200 leaflets addressed to places in those cities in the mails; and in Vienna an additional 400 were directed to Frankfurt am Main.

2. Sophia Scholl posted 200 in Augsburg and on another occasion 600 in Suttgart.

3. Hans Scholl, with the aid of Schmorell, scattered thousands of leaflets in the streets of Munich at night.

4. On February 18 the Scholls deposited 1500–1800 copies in bundles in the University of Munich, and Sophie Scholl let drop a large number from the third floor down the light well of the building.

Hans Scholl and Schmorell also, on the nights of August 8, 1942, and February 14, 1943, defaced walls in many places in Munich, and particularly the University, with the words "Down With Hitler," "Hitler the Mass Murderer," and "Freedom." After the first incident Sophia Scholl learned of this action, was in in agreement with it, and requested—though without success—to be allowed to help in the future!

Expenses were covered by the accused themselves— in all, about 1,000 marks.

Probst likewise began his medical studies in the spring of 1939 and is now in his eighth semester, a soldier on student duty. He is married and has three children aged two and a half, one and one fourth years, and four weeks. He is a "nonpolitical man"— hence no man at all! Neither the solicitude of the National Socialist Reich for his professional training nor the fact that it was only the National Socialist demographic policy which made it possible for him to have a family prevented him from writing at the behest of Scholl—in cowardly defeatism—a "manuscript" which takes the heroic struggle in Stalingrad as the occasion for defaming the Führer as a military swindler and which then, progressing to a hortatory tone, calls for opposition to National Socialism and for action which would lead, as he pretends, to an honorable capitulation. He supports the promises in this leaflet by citing—Roosevelt! And his knowledge about these matters he derived from listening to British broadcasts!

All the accused have admitted the facts stated above. Probst offers as excuse his "psychotic depression" of the time he drafted the leaflet, a depression which he claims arises from Stalingrad and the childbed illness of his wife. But such explanations do not excuse a reaction *of this scope.*

Whoever has, like the three accused, committed the acts of high treason, weakening the home front and thereby in time of war the security of the nation, and by the same token aids the enemy (Par. 5 of Special War Decree, and Par. 91b of the Criminal Code), raises the dagger for a stab in the back of the frontline troops! That applies also to Probst, though he claims that his manuscript was not intended for use as a leaflet—since the tone and style of the manuscript proves the opposite. Whoever acts in this way—and particularly at this time, when we must close our ranks—is attempting to cause the first rift in the unity of the battle front. And German students, whose traditional honor has always called for self-sacrifice for *Volk* and fatherland, were the ones who acted thus!

If a deed of this sort were to be punished otherwise than by death, we would be forging the first links of a chain whose end—in an earlier time—was 1918. Therefore, for the protection of the *Volk* and the Reich at war, the People's Court has found but one just punishment: death. The People's Court knows that it is at one with our soliders in this decision.

Through their treason to our *Volk*, the accused have forever forfeited their citizenship.

Everything found by the People's Court in this judgment is likewise a finding in the present action. The findings here, to the extent that the accused have complicity in those acts, are based on their own statements, as indeed all charges in this trial are founded on the statements of the accused themselves (except in those particular instances where we expressly point to other evidence). Only in the following points has the present trial resulted in a different view of the facts:

1. The leaflet "Students" was written by Huber. Scholl and Schmorell merely subjected it to minor rewriting (see below) and then published it.

2. In Stuttgart it was not Sophie Scholl but Hans Hirzel who put the leaflets in the mails. Sophie Scholl brought them to him in Ulm and requested him to prepare them for mailing and to place them in mailboxes in Stuttgart.

3. Grimminger contributed 500 marks toward their expenses. These errors in the first statement of charges resulted from the fact that the persons then accused took upon themselves the crimes of the three present accused (Huber, Hirzel, and Grimminger).

The People's Court, which is rendering judgment on this occasion with the same panel of senior and honorary judges as at that time, finds it significant that its judgment in the earlier trial would not have been different if it had known the truth on these three points.

Today the People's Court has had to render judgment on a second part of the core group in this organization:

1. Schmorell, who acted approximately in the same way as Scholl;

2. Graf, who collaborated treasonously and in aid of the enemy to almost the same degree as Schmorell and Scholl. Both had been assigned by the armed services to the study of medicine. Both ought to have been particularly grateful to the Führer, for he ordered army pay for them during the time of their university attendance—as was true for all enlistees assigned to medical study. Inclusive of money for food, they received over 250 marks per month, and exclusive of money for food, but with rations in goods, it still amounted to about 200 marks—more than most students ordinarily receive from home. Both were sergeants, both were assigned to student companies!

3. Alongside them is a man who is supposed to be an educator: the erstwhile Professor *Huber*, self-styled philosopher, a man whose influence on his students in his own specialty may have been good. (We have neither the need

125

nor the knowledge to judge his professional competence.) But a German university professor is first and foremost an educator of the young. As such he ought to try, in time of difficulty and struggle, to see that our university students are trained to be worthy younger brothers of the soldiers of 1914 at Langemarck in Flanders; that they are reinforced in their absolute trust in our Führer, our people and our Reich; and that they become seasoned fighters, prepared for any sacrifice!

The accused *Huber*, however, acted in an exactly opposite manner! He nourished doubt instead of dispelling it; he delivered addresses about federalism and democracy for Germany, about a multiparty system, instead of teaching and setting an example in his own life of rigorous National Socialism. It was not a time for tackling theoretical problems, but rather for grasping the sword, yet he sowed doubt among our youth. He helped to publish a treasonous leaflet of the "Resistance Movement," and he himself wrote another, entitled "Students." Admittedly, he strongly desired the retention of a sentence he had written, wherein he urged the student body to give their services unstintingly to the armed services. But the fact that he included this sentence does not exonerate him, for here he was playing the game of pitting the army against the Führer and the NSDAP, which was attacked and slandered most viciously later in the leaflet. Therefore the fact that the accused students deleted this sentence against his will does not excuse him in the least. Whoever tells the German army to turn against National Socialism intends to sap its strength. For the might of the army rests on the National Socialist philosophy of our soldiers. That is the basis of the indomitable strength of our National Socialist revolutionary troops! A "professor" of this sort — in the view of those great advocates of duty among all German academics, Fichte and Kant — is a blemish upon German scholarship, a blot which a few days ago was erased in connection with these proceedings. He was removed from his post in disgrace and was stripped of his professorial rights and privileges. Huber further states that he believed he was performing a good deed. But we will not relapse into the error of the

Weimar interregnum, which looked upon traitors as men of honor and safeguarded such so-called conscientious objectors by sending them off for detention in fortresses. The days when every man can be allowed to profess his own political "beliefs" are past. For us there is but one standard: the National Socialist one. Against this we measure each man!

Schmorell talks nonsense about his mother's being Russian and that he is therefore part Russian. He wanted somehow to bring Germans and Russians together; this was his excuse. The extent of bottomless confusion in which he finds himself is indicated by the statement he made at the principal trial that, as a German soldier, he had made up his mind "not to fire upon either Germans or Russians"! The National Socialist system of justice carefully investigates the personality of the accused. But these investigations can and should not enter into eccentric, unrealistic, and anti-German attitudes. The People's Court must ascertain above all that no such rift in time of war shall ever again be opened in our nation. Schmorell is a German soldier; he has taken his oath of duty to the Führer; he was allowed to continue his studies at the expense of the community at large. He has no right to any mental reservations about being half Russian. In any case, the morality of *reservatio mentalis* is not allowed in a German court.

Graf at least had the courage at the end of the principal trial to declare that there is no excuse for his crime. But his crime is so grave that this insight, coming so late, cannot alter the judgment.

In particular, the three accused committed the following acts:

1. Schmorell took counsel with Scholl about all that they did (apart from the leaflets of the White Rose and the draft by Probst—which are of no moment in these proceedings).

He had part in the decision to compose and distribute leaflets; he worked actively in their preparation; provided some of the needed equipment; knew of and accepted the contents of the leaflets, particularly the "Resistance Movement" and the agitational leaflet, "Students"; took part

127

in their distribution outside Munich and himself traveled to Salzburg, Linz, and Vienna; there mailed them to addresses in those cities and in Frankfurt; took part in the night-time scattering of leaflets and defacing of walls and in the distribution of leaflets through the mails in Munich; was present at a farewell party for himself and Graf in the studio of one Eickemayer (when they were about to depart for duty at the front in the summer of 1942); and attended other meetings with Huber and women students, where political discussions involving treasonous ideas and plans were held. Further, he traveled with Scholl to Grimminger, to obtain money from the latter; and, again with Scholl, to Harnack for purposes of recruiting.

2. The identical case can be laid against Graf, excepting only the trips outside of Munich and furnishing materials for the technical production of the leaflets. Instead, however, Graf took a trip for purposes of spreading information and recruiting; this trip led him to Bollinger, among others, whom he tried to win for his cause.

3. Huber knew of the work of Scholl, who had told him of his ideas, plans, and acts; he took part in the meetings, edited the leaflet "To All Germans" of the resistance; himself furnished the draft of the leaflet "Students" (see above); in meetings he stated his "political" position regarding the necessity of a federated South German democracy, as opposed to the alleged Prussian-Bolshevist wing of National Socialism, thus confirming the students in their enmity to the people and the state. The spirit in which he undertook these acts is shown incontrovertibly by his draft of the leaflet. It does not alter anything in his attitude and his actions that, as he says, he had wanted (but without success) to withdraw the draft after his remarks about the students and the army were deleted. For if the leaflet as he wrote it had been published, his behavior would have merited exactly the same judgment.

Whoever, as teacher or student, vilifies the Führer in this way no longer belongs to us. Whoever slanders National Socialism in this way no longer has a place among us. Whoever so splits our national unity and will to struggle in time of war, with the treasonable spawn from the brain of an enemy of the people, chips away at our armed security and gives aid to the enemy (Par. 91b of the Criminal Code). Men such as Huber, Schmorell, and Graf know this full well.

Whoever commits these acts has earned his death. No services (such as Huber alludes to) can extenuate his behavior.

As regards the significance of his activities, the accused Grimminger is most closely allied with this first group of sentenced persons — those who, with the Scholls and Probst (likewise sentenced in the first trial) formed the core of this stab-in-the-back organization of the so-called resistance movement. Scholl and Schmorell visited Grimminger in Stuttgart, told him of their agitation against the people and their plans for distributing leaflets and visiting universities for the purpose of finding collaborators. They told him that they wanted him to contribute money for these purposes. He replied evasively but did tell Scholl to come back after a few weeks. Scholl did so, and at that time Grimminger gave him 500 marks! To be sure, he did not give the impression that he knew he was helping to undermine the unity of the home front and weakening our armed security and thereby helping the enemy. But even if this must be counted a serious instance of treason, he would have been punished more severely if it had not been shown at the conclusion of the trial (testimony of the witness Hahn) that he did a great deal to help his employees who are in the army. He intends to support one of them, who has been severely wounded, through his university studies. All these considerations caused the court to place more credence in his statement that he had no intention of helping the enemy of the Reich, and it places his personality in a somewhat more favorable light. Accordingly, the People's Court has determined that his crime (Par. 83 of the Criminal Code) will be atoned for by ten years' imprisonment, through which sentence the security of the Reich so far as he is concerned will be fully guaranteed.

The next group of accused, Bollinger and Bauer, despite their knowledge of the treasonous anti-German activities, failed to report their information and in addition listened to the enemy.

Bollinger was acquainted with Graf through association with him in a Catholic Youth organization, *Das neue*

Deutschland, in the Saar before its return to the Reich. (Incidentally, Scholl was also a member of this group, so that Bollinger knew him also.)

When Graf, on the advice of Scholl, decided to use a trip to the Rhineland to sound out the opinions of acquaintances in the university towns of Bonn and Freiburg—and to recruit them for anti-German projects—he intended to meet Bollinger in Freiburg, but learned that the latter had gone to Ulm. There he sought him out, and the two of them visited Bollinger's acquaintances. With these people they did not discuss politics, but late at night, as Bollinger was seeing Graf off at the railroad station, Graf told him about the ideas and plans of the Scholl circle in Munich. Graf's attempts to recruit this man were unsuccessful, but apparently he gave him a copy of a leaflet, which Bollinger shortly thereafter showed to his friend, the accused Bauer, as well as to an acquaintance in the "Neues Deutschland" group! He did so, not in order to recruit, but to let Bauer know about Bollinger's conversation with Graf. Bollinger and Bauer were in agreement about their rejection of the leaflet and the entire Scholl action.

For the sake of the security of the Reich, we must render the judgment indicated above in order to show that, whoever as a mature adult with university training such as these two, fails to report a matter of this kind will end in prison. The police cannot be everywhere. The community will not prosper unless every man who considers himself a decent German supports the Party, the state, and the authorities and reports treasonous acts whenever he has knowledge of them. The disobedience of these two men toward the Führer deserves punishment, since, though they knew it to be forbidden by the Führer, they listened to discussions of military and internal political affairs on the foreign radio. This they did repeatedly on weekends together in a ski hut. They attempted to excuse themselves on the grounds that they wanted to learn only about the alleged student unrest in Munich. What a stupid and brazen excuse! A decent German does not gather information about such matters from Radio Beromünster or London!

The grave crime of failure to report high treason (Par. 139, Criminal Code) and listening to foreign broadcasts (Par. 1 of the Decrees concerning Special Radio Measures) has been punished by the Court with seven years' imprisonment for each man. To be sure, they both pleaded that their professional careers would be ruined, but they should have thought about that earlier!

Huber, Schmorell, and Graf, as traitors who aided the enemy in time of war and weakened our armed security, have acted in bad faith and have disgraced German youth— especially the youth who fought at Langemarck. Through their treason they have forfeited their honor forever. Further, Grimminger, Bollinger, and Bauer have forfeited their citizen's rights by their disloyalty for a period of time equal to the term of sentence, as the People's Court has determined.

The third group of accused in the present trial are foolish children, who present no serious threat to the security of the Reich.

At the head we find here the schoolmates Hans Hirzel and Franz Müller. Hirzel often visited Scholl when the latter was in Ulm on leave. Scholl exercised a strong influence and persuasiveness, particularly on such an immature addle-brain as Hirzel. And this power, as the People's Court knows from firsthand experience, was even heightened by the fact that it consisted of nothing but intellectualistic theorizing. Scholl worked on Hirzel for his purposes. He advised him to inform himself in political matters, so that at Germany's collapse he might work as a public speaker to promote Scholl's federalistic-individualistic multiparty democracy!

Sophie Scholl persuaded Hans Hirzel to distribute leaflets expressing these ideas. On two occasions she notified him in advance of her coming and asked him to meet her at the station. However, he wanted to avoid the meeting and did not show up; as a result she came to him, brought about 500 leaflets, and asked him to prepare them for mailing to addresses in Stuttgart. He copied names out of the city directory and put them in the mails. He agreed to and performed this action though on a later reading of the leaflets he could

131

not declare himself in agreement with their contents! The extent to which his mind was poisoned by the Scholls is shown by the fact that earlier he had accepted from them 80 marks for the purpose of buying a duplicating machine and equipment; that he further tried to make an anti-German poster—a swastika with the caption, "Whoever wears this is an enemy of the people." To be sure, he was unsuccessful in this, and he threw the duplicating machine into the Danube even before Sophie Scholl brought him the leaflets.

It has struck the Court that three pupils from one and the same school class (there was also Heinrich Guter) are involved in this action and that even more names were mentioned! There must be something at the bottom of all this, having to do with the atmosphere in this class and for which the Senate cannot hold these students alone to blame. One has to be ashamed that there is a class of this sort in a German humanistic *Gymnasium*! But it is not the job of the Court to investigate the underlying reasons in detail. The family of young Hirzel had wanted to raise him to be a decent German. Obviously he is not very well, he has had several serious bouts of illness, and he shows a tendency toward an exclusive preoccupation with intellectual matters, which in reality is more a dilettantish interest in phraseology and an urge to experiment. This boy, hardly aware of his own nature, came under the influence of a vile girl, Sophie Scholl, and let himself be misused. His confused attempts to philosophize, to explain his deeds, even though he was not in agreement with the leaflet, appeared not to be lies; they merely bore testimony to his conceit. The Court assumes that he will rid himself of this trait upon experiencing his moral awakening to the manhood of active life, as he will do with his eccentric—but in this connection characteristic—attempts to conduct experiments by injecting himself with chemicals or to have himself locked in a cement mixer so that he can observe the mixing process from the inside! We do not judge him by standards that apply to a university student or instructor.

The same holds for Franz Müller. He does not create the impression of illness, but he was also involved in less serious crimes. He succumbed to the pseudo intellectuality of Hirzel. His guilt consists in helping Hirzel on two occasions in the writing of addresses and in preparing the leaflets destined for Stuttgart for mailing.

The Court finds the two cases to be equal. Neither wanted to aid the enemy, though both understood that they were assisting high traitors in their crimes (Pars. 83, 49 of the Reich Criminal Code). Neither has cut himself off from the community of the *Volk* for all time. Hence on this ground neither would have to be sent to prison. But both of them deserve a prison sentence: firstly, so that they will come to understand their misdeeds and can be firmly indoctrinated; and secondly, so that other persons may not think they can be excused on grounds of immaturity. Five years' imprisonment for each would appear to the Court to be sufficient and appropriate.

The next group consists of the youths and girls who, though they refused to participate, nevertheless did not report the treason. This crime applies especially to the accused *Guter*. His classmate Hirzel had informed him of his intentions and acts. Guter refused to help. He also knew that Hirzel intended to travel to Stuttgart and place the leaflets in the mailboxes. On the very day of his return, Hirzel told Guter that he had done so. Guter excuses his failure to report this action on the ground of comradely feeling. Of course we want to train our youth to comradeship, but this is not the occasion for it. Comradeship does not hold for people who cut themselves off from the community by their anti-German acts. At this point higher duties toward society come into play. Guter's attorney claimed, of course, that Guter did not know the meaning of high treason. That extenuation needs no comment. In the eyes of the Court it is the same for him as for all the people—namely, a threat to the National Socialist way of life of the German people. That is all one needs to know. A high school student at the senior level must be well aware of it. He knows, too, that one has to notify the authorities of such acts. Therefore Guter had to be punished and was given a year and a half of imprisonment.

As a boy, Guter had a responsibility greater than the girls, but they also need to be punished for having failed to report treason. They are Katharina *Schüddekopf*, Gisela *Schertling*, and Traute *Lafrenz*. All, as they admit, knew of the crime of Scholl and Schmorell, though not in its details, but they made no report (Par. 139, Criminal Code). They are sentenced to a year's imprisonment.

The Schertling girl was very close to Scholl. Of course he tried to hide his treasonous acts from her, but on one occasion she happened to arrive just as quantities of leaflets, already prepared, were lying in view. (She testified: "Three army knapsacks full!") At that time she had to be let in on the secret. But she did not report it. On one occasion also she helped to distribute the leaflets, but the Court has not counted this as an especially serious matter, for it happened as follows: She went out with the Scholl girl. The latter was carrying a briefcase. Stopping at a mailbox, she opened the briefcase and began to throw in letters. To be of help, the Schertling girl raised the lid of the mailbox. That action came so suddenly and unexpectedly that at the moment the thought did not cross her mind that now she was helping to undermine the state, and the way in which she described the event in court indicates that, as she viewed it at the time, it was no more than a gesture of common courtesy. Nevertheless, the fact that she did not report the work of the Scholls has to be punished. The fact that in her relations with them she was thinking of something other than their treason does not excuse her.

Käte Schüddekopf and Traute Lafrenz also belonged, like the Schertling girls, to the group Scholl-Schmorell-Huber. They were present at their gatherings,—at the farewell party in the Eickemayer studio, for example, or at evening readings, where political discussions were carried on by these enemies of the people; where they slandered National Socialism and spoke of the necessity of taking action against it. The mere existence of a circle of that kind constitutes a treasonous threat to the Reich. They failed to report it. The Schüddekopf girl, who has given an impression of frankness and who came into the circle accidentally, also on one occasion passed along a leaflet to the Lafrenz girl. She did so, however, not, as the leaflets urge, in order to recruit, but in the assurance (which turned out to be justified) that the Lafrenz girl would not accept its message. Instead of passing it on, she destroyed it. In these circumstances the Court felt it should not find any element of treason in this receiving and passing on of the leaflet; yet, as we have said, the fact of failure to report remains.

The three girls have credibly testified that they have long since freed themselves from the influence of this traitorous activity and inwardly affirmed the National Socialist way of life of our people. This, too, has been noted by the Court in determining their sentence.

There remains Susanne *Hirzel*. She attended the music school in Stuttgart; she worked hard and made good progress in her studies. She was always a decent girl, raised at home to support the state, and was given a proper upbringing suited to a woman.

Unexpectedly her favorite brother Hans called her one day, arranged to meet her in town, and told her that he was coming without their parents' knowledge and that he had "letters" to mail. He was not in agreement with their contents, but there could be no harm in mailing them. Now she suspected, naturally, that there was something amiss, but she did not check over their contents, and she helped him post the "letters"—they were the leaflets "Students." Further, she took it upon herself to mail those that remained after her brother left.

Susanne Hirzel gives an impression of candor. The Court believes her when she says that she did not discover that her brother was engaged in treasonous activity. But it was inexcusable that she did not investigate further to check the actual contents of the package with the several hundred "letters," with their supposedly harmless internal-political content. Such would have been her duty. Because she did not follow it, she was sentenced to six months' imprisonment (Par. 85, Criminal Code).

All the accused who were sentenced to jail or to prison will have their terms of sentences shortened by the period of police and investigative custody, for they did not in any culpable way prolong that custody.

The accused *Harnack* came into the affair by accident.

He was a soldier in Chemnitz. One day two strangers, Scholl and Schmorell, came to see him; they had been sent to him by his fiancée, who was in Munich. At first he was pleased to have a message from her, but then they plied him with their anti-German ideas and plans and tried to recruit him for their purposes. When he refused, they left. Shortly afterward he visited his fiancée in Munich. At her suggestion he there met with Scholl and Schmorell again on two successive days. As against their democratic-individualistic ideas he defended the National Socialist program of a planned economy. Scholl and Schmorell (Huber was also present on the second occasion and argued on their side) declared this program to be communistic. They separated without coming to any agreement. Harnack was obligated to report this occurrence (Par. 139, Reich Criminal Code), but a little while before, he had undergone a very difficult personal experience with his brother and sister-in-law. The former had been sentenced to death for high treason by the Reich Military Court. Harnack himself had had no part in this affair, but he was still suffering from the shock that a sentence of this kind gave his family—a family of scholars well known throughout Germany. It is a unique case, which would not occur once in a hundred years in the German Reich, that almost immediately after the brother of an accused man is sentenced to death for treason the accused himself learns of another case of high treason. The judge must measure actions by a yardstick that applies to a strong man. However, the Court felt that even by this standard, it was not called upon to punish Harnack as a criminal, because of the special circumstances surrounding his case; that under the influence of his upsetting experience in the family (as the only adult male, he was obliged to provide also for the minor children of his brother) he simply did not measure up to the standard of strength and manhood that would make him conscious of his duty to report and would help him carry out such a resolve. He is industrious and highly talented, as the reports of his work as a student of theater attest. But it is of even greater significance that, as an artist, he is enthusiatically National Socialistic. This is

136

shown by his work at the Weimar National Theater and
in his productions for soldiers at the front. For this reason
it seemed proper that the Court not punish his omission.
The Reich is not harmed thereby, and the man is thus
justly treated, in accordance with his unique situation.
Therefore he has been set free.

The accused who have been sentenced will pay the
court costs.

However, the state will make good for the expenses
of the action against Harnack, since he has been acquitted.

Stier

signed
Dr. Freisler

DOCUMENT 4. Letter from Else Gebel, November 1946, to the Scholl Family Relating the Events and Scenes of Hans and Sophie Scholl's Days in Prison, February 18 to 22, 1943.*

To the Memory of Sophie Scholl.

I have before me your picture, Sophie, earnest, questioning, standing alongside your brother and Christoph Probst. It is as if you suspected what a heavy destiny you were to fulfill, which was to unite the three of you in death.

February 1943. As a political prisoner, I am put to work in the receiving office at the Gestapo headquarters in Munich. It is my job to register those other unfortunates who have fallen into the hands of the secret police and to record their personal data in the card catalogue which grows larger day by day.

For days now there has been feverish excitement among the officials. With increasing frequency at night the streets and houses are being painted with signs, "Down With Hitler!" "Long Live Freedom," or simply "Freedom."

At the University leaflets have been found strewn about the corridors and on the stairs. At the prison office there is a marked tenseness in the atmosphere. None of the investigative personnel come from the headquarters to the prison; most of them have been detailed on "Special Investigative Duty." Which of the brave fighters for freedom will they snare now? We who are familiar with the methods of these merciless brutes are torn with anxiety for the people who are daily apprehended.

Early on Thursday, February 18, there is a telephone call from headquarters: "Keep a number of cells free for today." I ask the official who is my boss who is expected, and he says, "The painters."

A few hours later, you, Sophie, are brought in by an

*In 1946 Else Gebel sent Inge Scholl the following detailed account of Sophie's last days and hours. Else Gebel was a political prisoner assigned to work duty at the Prison Administration of Gestapo Headquarters, Munich. She was Sophie's cellmate during the four days and nights that Sophie spent there. Sophie had elicited a promise from her fellow prisoners that they would relay the story of her last days to her parents.—ARS

Sophie Scholl

official to wait in the receiving room. You are quiet, relaxed, almost amused by all the excitement around you. Your brother Hans was brought in shortly before, and he has already been locked up. Every new arrival must hand over his papers and belongings and then submit to a bodily search. Since there are no female guards in the Gestapo, I have to perform this job. For the first time we stand face to face and alone, and I can whisper: "If you have a leaflet on you, destroy it now. I am a prisoner too."

Will you trust me, or do you think that the police are laying a trap? Your quiet, friendly manner allays all suspicion. You are not in the least excited. I can feel my own tension giving way. They must have made a big mistake in bringing you here. For surely this sweet girl with the innocent child's face has never been involved in such reckless acts.—You are even assigned the best cell, which is generally reserved for "deviationist" Nazi bigwigs. Its superiority consists of its having a larger window, containing a small locker, and having white covers on the blankets.

In the meantime I am ordered, while under surveillance, to get my belongings from the cell I have been in until now, and I am transferred to your cell. Again we are alone for a moment. You lie on the bed and ask how long I've been in detention and how I am getting along. Immediately you tell me that yours is probably an important case and therefore you will not be able to count on an easy outcome. Again I advise you under no circumstances to admit anything for which no evidence exists. "Yes, that is the way I behaved up to now at the university and at the preliminary examination before the Gestapo," you answer. "But there are so many things that they may be able to find." Steps approach the cell door, you are taken away for interrogation, I am sent to my work.

It is now close to three o'clock. Various other students, men and women, are brought in, but some of them are dismissed after a brief examination. Your brother Hans is already being interrogated. What may those men "up there" meanwhile have discovered in the way of incriminating evidence? It is six o'clock. Supper is brought, and you are conducted back to the cells, but separately. A servant, likewise a prisoner, brings warm soup and bread when the phone rings: "The two Scholls are not to have anything to eat; the examination will resume in half an hour." But down here we wouldn't think of withholding the food from you, and so you are both somewhat strengthened for the next interrogation. It is eight o'clock, and I have finished my last task, the "prison roster." Several more unfortunates have come to this house of suffering. About ten o'clock I go to bed and wait for your return. I lie awake and stare anxiously out into the clear, starry night. I try to pray for you in order to calm my nerves. In the evenings the officials whisper secretively with one another. Seldom does that presage anything good. Hour after hour goes by, and you do not return. Toward morning I am exhausted and fall asleep.

At 6:30 the servant brings in coffee. Usually at this time I am informed if anything has happened. Soon my hope that you might have been released after all is dashed. I learn that the two of you were under interrogation all night long, and toward morning you confessed; that the weight of evidence in their hands had brought you to this, after you denied everything for hours. Totally depressed, I go about my melancholy duties. I am fearful about the state of your spirit when you come down, and I hardly believe my eyes when, toward eight o'clock, you stand there absolutely calm, though tired. There, in the receiving room, I give you breakfast, and you tell me that they even gave you real coffee during the questioning. Then you are taken back to the cell, and I go along under the pretext that I have forgotten something. Before they have time to fetch me back, I have found out a number of things. You kept denying your complicity for a long time, but after all, at the university they found the text of a leaflet in Hans' pocket. Of course he had torn it up immediately and stated that it had come from a student whose name he didn't know. But the Gestapo agents had already made a thorough search of your rooms. They carefully pieced together the torn paper and found the handwriting to be the same as that of a friend of yours. Then the two of you knew that all was lost, and from that moment on all your thoughts were: We will take the blame for everything, so that no

141

other person is put in danger. They let you alone for a few hours, and you sleep well and deeply. I begin to be amazed at you. These many hours of interrogation have no effect on your calm, relaxed manner. Your unshakable deep faith gives you the strength to sacrifice yourself for the sake of others.

Friday evening. The whole afternoon you had to submit to many questions and frame your answers, but you are not in the least fatigued. You tell me about the impending invasion, which must occur in eight weeks at the latest. Then Germany will receive blow upon blow, and at last we will be released from tyranny. Of course I am ready to believe you, but I am troubled by the fear that you will no longer be with us. You doubt that you will live to see that day, but when I tell you how long they have held my brother without bringing him to trial—more than a year now—you begin to have hope. In your case it will certainly take a long time. Gain time and you gain everything.

Today you tell me how often you scattered leaflets at the university, and in the face of the gravity of the situation, we laugh when you tell how once on the way home from a "scattering tour" you went up to a charwoman who wanted to gather up the leaflets from the steps and said to her. "Why do you pick up those sheets? Just let them lie there; the students are supposed to read them." Then again: how well you knew at all times that if ever the agents of the Gestapo caught one of you, it would cost your life. I can understand that often you were in exultant high spirits when you had completed a night's work, hanging banners in the streets or placing a stack of letters of the "White Rose" in mailboxes to await their delivery. If you happened to have a bottle of wine, you opened it in celebration of one of your successes.

You also describe for me your last action together. You and Hans have scattered the greater part of the leaflets in the university hall and are standing with your suitcase out in the Ludwigstrasse again when you decide that it ought to be possible to empty the bag before you go home. On the spur of the moment you turn around, go back into the hall and up to the top of the stairs, and fling the remaining sheets down the light well. Naturally this causes a commotion, and the Gestapo officers order all the doors locked. Every person has to show his papers. All of a sudden the corridors are completely empty. As you come down the staircase, the custodian Schmiedel [sic] comes toward you, to hand you over to the Gestapo. On this evening we talk until late at night. I am unable to get to sleep, but you are breathing deep and rhythmically.

Saturday morning brings you more hours of interrogation. And when I come in at noon, glad to be able to tell you that now you will be left in peace until Monday morning, it doesn't please you at all. You find the questioning stimulating, interesting. At least you have the good fortune to have one of the few likable investigators. He— Mohr is his name—gave you a long lecture this morning about the meaning of National Socialism, the Führer principle, German honor, and how grievously you had compromised Germany's armed security by your deeds. Perhaps he wants to offer you one more chance when he asks, "Fräulein Scholl, if you had known and thought over all these things that I have now explained to you, you certainly would never have let yourself be swept along into acts of this kind, would you?" And what is your answer, you courageous, honest girl? "You are wrong. I would do exactly the same the next time, for it is you, not I, who have the mistaken *Weltanschauung*."

On this Saturday and Sunday we are served meals by prisoners detailed to these tasks. I have the utensils for brewing tea and coffee, and each of us contributes his bit. In our little cell we quickly accumulate the rarest riches— cigarettes, cookies, sausages, and butter. From our stocks we can also send things upstairs to your brother, about whom you worry so. We also send Willi Graf a cigarette with "Freedom" written on it.

Sunday morning brings you a great shock. At breakfast they whisper to me, "Last night another one of the principals in this action arrived." I tell you, and you think of none other than Alexander Schmorell. When at ten o'clock I am fetched for duty in the office, the entries for the previous night have already been registered, and the cards are already filed. I look them up and read: "Christoph

Probst. Treason." For two hours I am happy, knowing I'll be able to tell you that it isn't Alex whom they have caught, but I read horror in your face when I mention Christl's name. For the first time I see you upset. Christl—the good, true friend, father of three small children, the man who for the sake of his family you expressly did not want to involve—has now been drawn into the whirlpool because of this one leaflet. But you get hold of yourself again; at most they can give Christl a prison sentence, and he will soon have that behind him. At noon the investigator comes, and he brings fruit, cookies, and a couple of cigarettes, and asks me how you are feeling. Surely he is expressing pity, for he knows better than anyone else the black clouds that have gathered over your head. In the afternoon we sit together in our cell, until you are summoned (it is about three o'clock) to receive the notice of indictment. I am told that the proceedings against the three of you will begin tomorrow. The dreaded People's Court is in session here, and Freisler and his brutal accomplices are determined to pronounce sentence of death.

Dear, dear Sophie, your fate has already been decided. After a few minutes you come back, pale and very upset. Your hand trembles as you begin to read the bulky indictment. But the further you read, the calmer your expression becomes, and by the time you reach the end, your nervousness is dispelled. "Thank God," is all that you say. Then you ask me whether I can read the document with impunity, without risking some unpleasantness. Even in this hour you do not want anyone to risk danger on your account. You dear, pure soul, how I have come to love you in these last few days!

Outside it is a sunny February day. People pass by these walls happy and cheerful, not suspecting that once again three courageous, honest Germans are being handed over to their death. We have lain down on our beds, and in a soft, calm voice you begin to reminisce. "It is such a splendid, sunny day, and I have to go. But how many have to die on the battlefield in these days, how many young, promising lives. . . . What does my death matter if by our acts thousands of people are warned and alerted. Among the

144

student body there will certainly be a revolt." Oh, Sophie, you haven't learned how cowardly the human herd is! "After all, I could die of illness, but would that mean the same thing?" I try to hold out to you the hope that it might very well happen that you'll get by with a long prison sentence. But you, my faithful sister, will not let me talk about that. "If my brother is sentenced to death, then I must not and ought not to receive a lighter sentence. My guilt is exactly the same as his." You explain this also to your defense counsel, who has been brought in as a formality. He asks you whether you have any request. As if a puppet of his sort could see to it that any request was granted! No, you want only to have him confirm the fact that your brother has a right to execution by firing squad, for after all, he has been a frontline soldier. But even on this point he is unable to give you a definite answer, and he is horrified at your further question, as to whether you are likely to be publicly hanged or are to die on the guillotine. That sort of question, asked in such a calm way, and by a young girl—he hadn't expected this. Where ordinarily strong men who are used to battle would tremble, you remain quiet and composed. But naturally he gives you evasive answers.

Mohr stops in again to advise you to write your letters to your loved ones today if possible, since in Stadelheim prison they'll let you write only brief notes. Are his intentions kindly, or do they hope to obtain new evidence from the letters? In any case, your family have never been allowed to read as much as a line of those letters. After ten o'clock we go to bed. You continue to tell me about your parents and brothers and sisters. Concern for your mother oppresses you. To lose two children at the same moment, and the other brother on duty somewhere in Russia! "Father has a better understanding of what we did." All night long the light is kept on, and every half-hour an officer comes to see that everything is still in order. These people have no conception of your deep faith, your trust in God! The night stretches out endlessly for me, while you sleep soundly as always.

Shortly before seven o'clock I have to wake you for this difficult day. You wake at once and tell me, still seated on the bed, about your dream: On a beautiful sunny day you brought a child in a long white dress to be baptized. The way to the church was up a steep mountain, but you carried the child safely and firmly. Unexpectedly there opened up before you a crevice in the glacier. You had just time enough to lay the child safely on the other side before you plunged into the abyss. You interpreted your dream this way: "The child in the white dress is our idea; it will prevail in spite of all obstacles. We were permitted to be pioneers, but we must die early for the sake of that idea." I will have to go to the office soon. How I hope for your safety, how my thoughts will constantly be with you, you undoubtedly know. I promise you that later, in quieter times, I will tell your parents about our days together. Then a last handshake: "God be with you, Sophie"; and I am called away.

Shortly after nine o'clock they take you in a private car, accompanied by two officials, to the Palace of Justice. As you pass, you send me one last glance. Your brother Hans and Christoph Probst, both handcuffed, are also brought out and taken in another car.

Down here the prison seems deserted today. Instead of the coming and going of many people of the last days there is oppressive silence. After two o'clock we receive the frightful news from the headquarters: all three sentenced to death!

Paralyzed with fear, I hear the frightful report. Poor, dear Sophie, I wonder how you are bearing up. They say you were brave and not intimidated at the trial. May God give you the strength to hold out. Perhaps a plea for mercy will now succeed after all! Your friends and loved ones will try every possible means of saving you. Again I begin to hope a little. But the People's Court can set aside any and every traditional right.

At 4:30 Mohr comes in. He is still in his hat and coat, white as chalk. I am the first to ask, "Herr Mohr, is it really true that all three will die?" He only nods, himself still shaken by the experience. "How did she take the sentence? Did you have a chance to talk to Sophie?" In a tired voice he answers, "She was very brave; I talked with her in

Stadelheim prison. And she was permitted to see her parents." Fearfully I ask, "Is there no chance at all for a plea of mercy?"

He looks up at the clock on the wall and says softly, in a dull voice, "Keep her in your thoughts during the next half hour. By that time she will have come to the end of her suffering."

These words fall like bludgeon blows on all of us. We are stunned to learn that three good, innocent persons have to die because they dared to rise against an organized band of murderers, because they wanted to help to end this senseless war. I should like to scream these things at the top of my lungs, and I have to sit there silent. "Lord, have mercy on them, Christ have mercy on them, Lord have mercy on their souls," is all I can think. The minutes stretch to an eternity. I want to push the hands of the clock ahead, faster, faster, so that the heaviest task will be behind you. But one minute creeps slowly after the other.

Finally it is five o'clock; 5:04; 5:08.

You have returned into the light. May the Lord give you eternal rest, and may the eternal light shine upon you.

Else Gebel

November, 1946

Document 5. Article in the *Münchener Neueste Nachrichten* for Monday, February 22, 1943, Reporting the Sentencing and Execution of Hans and Sophie Scholl and Christoph Probst.

Death Sentences

For Preparation to Commit Treason

LPM. On February 22, 1943, the People's Court, convened in the Court of Assizes Chamber of the Palace of Justice, sentenced to death (together with loss of the rights and privileges of citizenship) the following persons: Hans Scholl, aged 24, and Sophia Scholl, aged 21, both of Munich, and Christoph Probst, aged 23, of Aldrans bei Innsbruck, for their preparations to commit treason and their aid to the enemy. The sentence was carried out on the same day.

Typical outsiders, the condemned persons shamelessly committed offenses against the armed security of the nation and the will to fight of the German *Volk* by defacing houses with slogans attacking the state and by distributing treasonous leaflets. At this time of heroic struggle on the part of the German people, these despicable criminals deserve a speedy and dishonorable death.

DOCUMENT 6. Article in the *Völkischer Beobachter*, Munich edition, for Wednesday, April 21, 1943, Reporting the Sentencing of Alexander Schmorell, Kurt Huber, Wilhelm Graf, and others.

Just Punishment of Traitors to the Nation at War

LPM. The People's Court of the German Reich, in session in Munich, dealt with a number of accused persons who were involved in the high treason of the brother and sister Scholl sentenced on February 22, 1943.

At the time of the arduous struggle of our people in the years 1942–43, Alexander Schmorell, Kurt Huber, and Wilhelm Graf of Munich collaborated with the Scholls in calling for sabotage of our war plants and spreading defeatist ideas. They aided the enemy of the Reich and attempted to weaken our armed security. These accused, having through their violent attacks against the community of the German people voluntarily excluded themselves from that community, were punished by *death*. They have forfeited their rights as citizens forever.

Eugen Grimminger of Stuttgart furnished funds in support of this action, though, to be sure, he was not fully aware of its details. The Court was unable to establish that he consciously gave aid to the enemy of the Reich. Furthermore, he gave considerable assistance to his employees who were serving in the armed forces, though on the other hand he was aware that the money might be used for purposes injurious to the state. He has been sentenced to ten years in jail. Heinrich Bollinger and Helmut Bauer of Freiburg had knowledge of the treasonous acts of the above-named accused but failed to report them, despite the fact that they are mature adults, and in contravention of the obligation of ˌevery German to make report of treasonous plans of this sort. In addition, they listened to enemy broadcasts. They have been sentenced to seven years in jail, and they have forfeited their honor as citizens for the same length of time.

Hans Hirzel and Franz Müller of Ulm, immature youths, aided in the distribution of the treasonous leaflets. In consideration of their youth they were sentenced to five years' imprisonment.

149

The accused Heinrich Guter of Ulm, likewise a young person who knew of the treasonous acts but failed to report them, was sentenced to eighteen months' imprisonment. Three girls who were guilty of the same act were sentenced to one year's imprisonment.

One other accused person, who assisted in the distribution of the leaflets but who did not know their contents, was given a sentence of six months in jail because she failed to carry out her obligation to inform herself about the contents of the leaflets.

DOCUMENT 7. Extract From a Letter from Bishop Berggrav, Oslo, to Inge Scholl, September 30, 1952, Relating How He Received the News of the Execution of Hans and Sophie Scholl.

Dear Inge Scholl:

From Charles Carroll I received the copy of *The White Rose* with your kind dedication. I should like to convey to you how deeply this moves me. I want to tell you: Some weeks after the dramatic events in Munich I was sitting in the evening with Count Helmuth von Moltke in Oslo (I was heavily disguised, as at the time I was a prisoner and had slipped out by taking advantage of the negligence of the guards). We were engaged in translating a radio broadcast from Munich into English for later retransmission to London, via Stockholm. Count Moltke's account was most moving, and the names of the Scholls have become sacred in my memory.

Eivind Berggrav

DOCUMENT 8. Excerpt from the Radio Series "German Listeners" ("Deutsche Hörer") by Thomas Mann, June 27, 1943, Referring to the Resistance of the Munich Students.

I say to you: Respect the peoples of Europe! Let me add, though at the moment it may sound strange to many of you who are listening, pay respect to the German people and show sympathy with them! The idea that it is impossible to distinguish between the German *Volk* and Nazism—that to be German and National Socialist are one and the same thing—is heard at times in the Allied countries, and put forward with some passion. But this idea is untenable and will not prevail. Too many facts testify to the contrary. Germany has set up its defenses and continues to resist, exactly as the other nations do. . . .

Now the world is deeply moved by the events at the University of Munich, about which we have received information through the Swiss and Swedish newspapers, at first imprecisely and then with particulars that fascinate us more and more. We know now about Hans Scholl, survivor of the Battle of Stalingrad, and his sister. We know of Adrian [*sic*] Probst, Professor Huber, and all the others;* about the Easter demonstration of students against the obscene speech of a Nazi bigwig in the *auditorium maximum;* we know of their martyrdom on the block; about the leaflet which they had distributed and which contains words that go far to make up for many of the sins against the spirit of German freedom committed in these unhappy years at the German universities. Indeed, this susceptibility of German youth—the youth in particular—to the National Socialist revolution of lies was painful. Now their eyes are opened, and they put their young heads on the block for their insight and for the honor of Germany. They go to their death after telling the president of the court to his face, "Soon you will be standing here, where I now stand," after bearing witness

---

*By Adrian Probst Mann means Christoph Probst. This error is undoubtedly due to the difficulties attendant on the transmission of news bulletins. The same holds for the remark that Hans Scholl was a veteran of the Battle of Stalingrad. — I.S.

in the face of death that a new faith in freedom and honor is dawning.

Good, splendid young people! You shall not have died in vain; you shall not be forgotten. The Nazis have raised monuments to indecent rowdies and common killers in Germany—but the German revolution, the real revolution, will tear them down and in their place will memorialize these people, who, at the time when Germany and Europe were still enveloped in the dark of night, knew and publicly declared: "A new faith in freedom and honor is dawning."

DOCUMENT 9. Text of a Leaflet Issued by the National Committee for a Free Germany, Addressed to the German Fighting Forces on the Eastern Front. *

Lower the flags

over the fresh graves
of German freedom fighters!

A short time ago we heard the terrible news that three young Germans, Hans and his sister Sophie Scholl and Christoph Probst, were executed at the end of February.

The three belonged to the group of noble and courageous spokesmen for German youth who refused to witness any longer the terrible sufferings of their Fatherland in non-committal and silent acceptance.

They were students at the University of Munich. Hans Scholl had returned just a few months before on study leave from the eastern front. He had been a valiant soldier and had received the Purple Heart, the Iron Cross Second Class, and the Eastern Front Medal.

Under Hans Scholl's leadership the Munich students were the first to raise the flag of freedom. They distributed leaflets and organized impressive demonstrations
against Gestapo terror and the betrayal of the masses;

---

*The National Committee for a Free Germany was set up among German army enlisted men taken as prisoners of war in Russia after their defeat at Stalingrad. Its purpose was to overthrow the Hitler regime by encouraging resistance, sabotage, and rebellion. The Committee was founded in the summer of 1943 in Moscow, and its initial manifesto was published on July 13.

Bodo Scheurig, in his recent study of the history of the committee (*Free Germany*, published in an English translation by Herbert Arnold, Wesleyan University Press, 1969), shows that the first leaflets and radio broadcasts directed to the German armed forces were prepared after July 13, 1943, and that by July 1944 the activity of the committee ceased. The present undated leaflet dealing with the fate of the Scholls was probably not prepared before midsummer of 1943. It may have been issued any time up to July 1944. —ARS against total mobilization, which reduces the German people to total misery;

against the debauched and dissipated high-echelon carousers of the SS, the SA, and the Hitlerian big-wigs;

against warmongers and prolongers of the war who, in their insatiable greed for profit or in stubborn fanaticism, let millions of Germans bleed to death;

against the whole arbitrary Hitler regime, which is out to achieve world rule and the enslavement of peoples, which has brought down upon Germany the infinite sufferings of total war, mass air raids, ruin, and misery;

against Hitler, the betrayer of peoples, the mad self-styled general, who through his quixotic policy of conquest, his fomenting of racial hate and bloody terrorizing of the occupied areas, has incited the hatred of the nations against Germany; who has ruined and decimated the German family, the German farmer and the middle classes; who has caused Germany to be overrun with foreign nationals; who has crushed and undermined the foundations of our existence and halted the processes of our historical growth.

These were the slogans of the demonstrating youth in Munich in February 1943.

The demonstrations were broken up by the SS. Several students were arrested, brutally mistreated, and haled before the Military Court.

They were called a "Threat and Danger to the German *Volk*" and "Communists."

"I am no communist; I am a German," stated Hans Scholl before the Court.

And as a German, as a soldier at the front, as a man with concern for the fate of his homeland and his people, this brave young freedom fighter defied his judges.

"You can execute me, but the day will come when you will be judged. The people, our German homeland will judge you!"

The ax of the Hitler executioner was raised three times; three times it descended; and three young heads rolled from the block.

Three heroes died, but their spirit, their love and their

hate, their struggle for peace and German freedom lives on in the hearts of hundreds of thousands and millions of young Germans. . . .

The renown of the brave is eternal.

Ulm—the home of the Scholls—and Munich—where they fought and died—will one day dedicate monuments in gratitude and respect to these heroes.

"Germany puts its hopes in its youth!" said Scholl in his last speech.

"As once in the Wars of Liberation in 1813–1814, now again German youth must rescue the fatherland from dishonorable tyranny, shame, misery, and war exploitation," added his sister.

Young Germans in uniform: Heed the call of alarm of the heroes of freedom from distant Munich. There speaks to you the voice of your unhappy homeland.

The most evil enemies and destroyers of Germany stand behind you. Yes, they give you your orders and incite you to self-destructive, utterly dangerous warfare.

Know the truth. Know the real enemy!

You alone can save our people, our homeland, from ruin and misery.

Officers and Soldiers: Do not be misled by lying, inflammatory slogans. Follow your own reason, your conscience, and your love for country.

For a free and peaceful Germany!

For the preservation and security of the German people, the German family!

Fight against the Hitler war and the Himmler terror!

Fight against Göring-Krupp war profiteering and Goebbels-Ley lies!

Fight against the enmity between nations and total war!

Bring the war to an end. Bring Hitler down!

German Youth, awake!

As in the case of the talk by Thomas Mann, there occur a number of errors in this document as a result of difficulties in news reporting. Except for a meeting in the Deutsches Museum in Munich, which had been called by Gauleiter Giessler and which

156

was disrupted by students in the audience, there were no "demonstrations." Further, the charge allegedly made in court that the accused were Communists, and the reply by Hans Scholl, cannot be verified. Whether the latter ever was awarded the military decorations which are mentioned is not known. The fact is that Nazi citations of this kind would have been unacceptable to him and to many anti-Fascists. Hans Scholl would (as on one occasion he admiringly referred to the example of Colonel Lawrence) have hung these medals on the tail of the first available dog.—I.S.

Document 10. Extract from a Letter from Kurt R. Grossmann,* New York, to Inge Scholl, Describing the Mass Meeting Held in New York in 1943, to Pay Tribute to the Six Victims of Nazi Punishment, the Schools, Probst, Schmorell, Huber, and Graf.

The year was 1943, a dreadful year since day by day the news from Europe represented tragedy, hoplessness, blood and tears. You recall: the extermination machine of the Nazis worked night and day. The only visible hope came from the Eastern front. The Germans had lost at Stalingard. Was it the beginning of the end? When would it come?

In New York there existed an organization, American Friends of Germany. Its instigators were political refugees belonging to the socialist group New Beginning (Neu-Beginnen), which opposed the policy of the pre-Hitler Social Democratic party of Germany. They distributed material on persecution, on political resistance, on trials in the Nazi Reich, attempting to analyze the political situation, publishing an excellent book and article survey, in short, keeping American liberals informed. I visited quite often the office picking up material, lending books, talking to Paul Hagen, its spiritual motor. One day he told me of the tragedy of your brother and sister, Sophie and Hans Scholl, their trial and death sentences. You have movingly described their deeds in your exciting book *Die Weisse Rose* (*Students against Tyranny*) and the "Geschwister Scholl" and their comrades have become historical figures. Hagen told me that a protest meeting was being planned at Hunter College for these Germans. "The Americans must learn to distinguish between Nazis representing the evil spirit and

---

*Kurt R. Grossmann (b. 1897) is a refugee author and publicist who came to the United States in 1939. After 1952 he was executive assistant of the Jewish Agency for Israel until his retirement on April 1, 1966. Grossmann is especially known as the Secretary General of the German League for Human Rights (1926–1933) and author of the first biography of Carl von Ossietzky (Kindler, Munich, 1963) for which he received the Albert Schweitzer Book Award. His latest book is *Emigration, The History of the Hitler Refugees 1933–1945* (Europäische Verlagsanstalt, Frankfurt, 1969).

'the other Germany' representing democracy." Three weeks later my wife and I attended this meeting at Hunter College, which remains unforgotten for several reasons.

Hundreds and hundreds of New Yorkers came to pay tribute to six heroic victims of the "other Germany." Their names meant little to them at that time but their deeds very much. Their sacrifice proved that Hitler was not the master of all Germans and their conscience; there was resistance, and their tragic death represented a glimmer of hope for the future. Two of the speakers were extraodinary personalities. The First Lady of the Land, Eleanor Roosevelt, wife of the President, spoke and she demonstrated then what she later wrote to me: "I like the Germans, especially those fighting Nazism, but I hate and despise the Nazis." Her speech was moving and of great political significance. Another speaker was one of the leading Negro women, Anna Hedgman (she later became a figure in the New York City administration under Robert F. Wagner). She spoke in the name of all suppressed people, she cried out and accused the oppressors, and like Eleanor Roosevelt she stretched out her hand to the brave resistance fighters in Germany. It was a moving, an exciting, yes a unforgettable evenning.

It happened in New York in the middle of the war — and this was the important message it relayed to the German people:

You must fight for your own liberty —

Like Sophie and Hans Scholl did.

When you, Inge, visited New York in April 1957 I had the idea to arrange a meeting with the speakers and organizers of this memorable Hunter College Meeting. However it was impossible to get even the most important participants together. Though you met at parties and meetings some of them connected, or not, with the event, we both cherish the memory of our tea with Mrs. Eleanor Roosevelt in the garden of her city residence at 211 East 62nd Street on April 29, 1957. The always gracious lady, on April 30, 1957, sent me a thank-you for the carnations, which concludes: "I am so glad you and Mrs. Aicher-Scholl could come in to see me yesterday."

Source: Letter to Inge Aicher-Scholl, March 15, 1969, with additions March 30, 1970. Reproduced by permission of its writer.

DOCUMENT 11. Extract from the Address by President Heuss of the Federal Republic of Germany to the Students of Berlin and Munich on the Occasion of the Memorial Ceremony Held on February 22, 1953.

When, ten years ago we learned—first in the form of a rumor and later reliably confirmed—of the bold attempt of the Scholls and their friends to touch the conscience of university students, we recognized and stated: This cry of the German soul will echo through history. Death cannot now, nor could it then, compel this outcry to silence. Their words, sent fluttering on sheets of paper through the hall of the University of Munich, were and have remained a beacon.

The courageous death of these young people, who pitted integrity of mind and courage to voice the truth against empty rhetoric and the lie, became a victory at the moment when their life was cut off.

This is how we must understand their appearance in in the midst of the German tragedy: not as an unsuccessful attempt to bring about change in the face of force, but rather as the extinguishing of a light shining in the darkest night.

For this we express our gratitude and honor their memory.

Theodor Heuss

Inge Scholl is the surviving sister of Hans and
Sophie Scholl.

Dorothee Sölle is the author of a number of books,
including *Suffering* and *Beyond Mere Obedience*. She is
Visiting Lecturer at Union Theological School in
New York City and Lecturer at the University of Hamburg, West Germany. She lives in Hamburg.

Arthur R. Schultz was Professor of German at Wesleyan
University from 1946 to 1979. He lives in Middletown,
Connecticut.